Culinary Art

Recipes from Great Chicago Restaurants

Culinary Art

Recipes from Great Chicago Restaurants

*Illustrated with works of art
from the collections of*

The Art Institute of Chicago

With recipes from

Bêtise · New Japan · Restaurant on the Park
Va Pensiero · Prairie · Frontera Grill
Papagus Greek Taverna · The Berghoff

Introduction and captions by

Tom Fredrickson

THE ART INSTITUTE OF CHICAGO

BETISE

Plaza del Lago, 1515 Sheridan Road, Wilmette

Raspberry-Stuffed French Toast with Warm Berry Compote

Salade Pas Bête

Balsamic Roasted New Potatoes

Pan-Fried Salmon with Red-Wine Vinegar and Mushrooms

Classic Crème Brûlée Bêtise

Fresh Peach and Ginger Cobbler with a Lemon-Biscuit Top

Bonnard

Few artists have expressed a household's meaning and intimacy as **Pierre Bonnard** did. He often painted scenes in and around the modest home near Cannes he shared with his lifelong companion and wife, Marthe. "Our life here is quite solitary and as routine as possible," he told a friend. While many of Bonnard's paintings exhibit an exquisite richness and almost hedonistic charm, *Still Life: Preparation for Lunch*—painted around 1940, when the artist was 73 years old—conveys an autumnal sense of stillness and solitude.

PAN-FRIED SALMON WITH
RED-WINE VINEGAR AND MUSHROOMS

2 tablespoons peanut oil

*4 salmon fillets, each 5 ounces, rinsed and
    patted dry*

salt and freshly ground pepper to taste

²/₃ cup red-wine vinegar

*16 medium mushrooms, sliced, with stems
    trimmed*

3 tablespoons butter

Heat the oil in a 10-inch, nonstick skillet over medium-high heat. Season the salmon
with salt and pepper. When the oil is hot, cook the fish skin side up until well-
browned, about 4 minutes. Gently turn with spatula. Cook, covered, until the
salmon is just cooked through; timing will depend on the thickness of the fillets.
Transfer the fish to four warm dinner plates. Keep the plates in a warm oven while
finishing the sauce.

   Pour the vinegar into the skillet and stir well with a wooden spoon. Add the
mushrooms and simmer until just tender, about 3 minutes. Remove from heat. Stir
in the butter until melted. Adjust the seasonings and spoon the sauce over the fish.
Serve immediately. *Serves 4.*

In 1908 **Henri Matisse** wrote that he wanted his paintings
to have "a soothing, calming influence on the mind, something...that provides relaxation from physical fatigue."
The subject of *Lorette with a Cup of Coffee* is steeped in
relaxation: An Italian model named Lorette—whom Matisse
painted over fifty times in 1916 and 1917—lazes on the floor
wearing a loose chemise; a china cup rests atop a small,
Moroccan-style table beside her. At once spontaneous
and carefully composed, this painting's mix of sensuality,
exoticism, and cozy domesticity is found in many of
Matisse's works.

CLASSIC CREME BRULEE BETISE

The fine linen, sugar bowl, empty tea cup, and goblet of wine in **Henri Fantin-Latour**'s *Still Life: Corner of a Table,* 1873, appeared a year earlier in his painting *The Corner Table* (Paris, Musée d'Orsay). Seated around the table in that earlier work are several major artists of the day, including the French Symbolist poets Paul Verlaine and Arthur Rimbaud. In the 1873 composition, Fantin-Latour focused on a few choice details to deftly suggest the elegance, luxury, and ease enjoyed by the artist and his circle.

5 large egg yolks

³/₄ cup sugar

1¹/₂ cups whipping cream

¹/₄ vanilla bean, split

Preheat the oven to 350°F. In a mixing bowl, whisk together the yolks and ¹/₄ cup of the sugar. Place the cream in a saucepan and scrape the vanilla bean over it. Add the vanilla bean and place over medium heat just until the cream simmers. Remove from heat and let stand 5 minutes.

While stirring, pour the warm cream into the yolk-sugar mixture. Pour the mixture through a fine-mesh strainer and ladle into four 6-ounce ramekins. Place the ramekins in a pan and fill the pan with 1 inch of water. Bake until the centers of the custards jiggle but are not runny, about 25 to 30 minutes. Allow to cool completely.

To serve, sprinkle the tops generously with the remaining sugar and broil until the sugar caramelizes. Rotate the crème brûlées a few times so they broil evenly. Watch carefully to keep the sugar from burning. *Serves 4.*

The late 18th and 19th centuries saw the advent of public restaurants. For the first time, the food of skilled cooks—previously a privilege only of nobility—was available to middle-class diners. The scene of **Pierre Auguste Renoir**'s *Rowers' Lunch,* 1875/1876, is the Restaurant Fournaise in Châtou, a Parisian suburb on the Seine. The fruit and liquor bottles (several of them empty) indicate that lunch has been finished and the diners are enjoying the leisure—smoking a cigar or watching passing skullers and other rowers—that outdoor dining at such restaurants allowed.

To the Victorians who collected paperweights, fruit and flowers carried specific symbolic meanings. Peaches were understood to indicate that "your qualities, like your charms, are unequaled." This rare, crystal object was created by the **Compagnie des Cristalleries de Saint-Louis**, one of the foremost makers of paperweights in the mid-1800s.

FRESH PEACH AND GINGER COBBLER
WITH A LEMON-BISCUIT TOP

COBBLER:

1³/₄ pounds firm, ripe peaches, peeled

¹/₄ cup sugar

1¹/₂ teaspoons fresh grated ginger or
  ¹/₂ teaspoon dried ginger

3 tablespoons flour

2 tablespoons dark rum

BISCUIT TOP:

1¹/₂ cups flour

¹/₂ teaspoon salt

1¹/₂ tablespoons sugar

2¹/₄ teaspoons baking powder

1¹/₂ tablespoons grated lemon zest

6 tablespoons unsalted butter

³/₄ cup whipping cream

2 tablespoons whipping cream

2 tablespoons sugar

whipped crème fraîche or vanilla ice cream as
  an accompaniment

Preheat the oven to 400°F. Slice the peaches into a bowl. Toss with the sugar, ginger, flour, and rum. Divide into six individual baking dishes.

Prepare the biscuit topping. Mix the dry ingredients in a bowl. Cut in the butter until the mixture looks like coarse cornmeal. Add the ³/₄ cup of whipping cream and mix gently just until ingredients are moistened.

Roll the dough out on a floured surface to a thickness of about ¹/₃ inch. Cut the dough to fit the tops of the baking dishes and lay on top of the peaches. Brush the dough with 2 tablespoons whipping cream and sprinkle with sugar.

Bake the cobblers until lightly browned, about 15 minutes. Serve warm with whipped crème fraîche or vanilla ice cream. *Serves 4.*

Chapter Two

JAPANESE

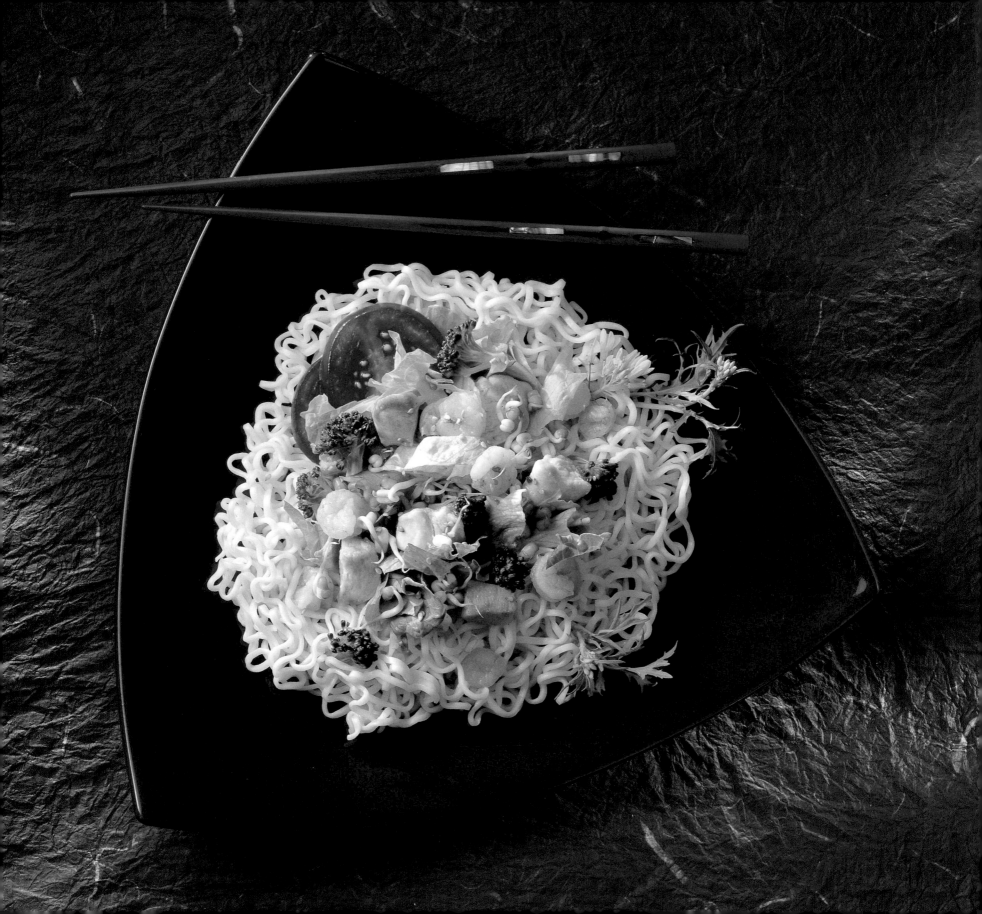

NEW JAPAN

1322 Chicago Avenue, Evanston

Miso-Shiru (Miso Soup)

Spinach Goma-ae (Spinach Salad with Sesame-Seed Dressing)

Age Dashi-Tofu (Deep-Fried Tofu with Tempura Sauce)

Teba-Karaage (Fried Chicken Wings)

Yakisoba (Stir-Fried Noodles)

Hiyashi-Chuka Soba (Cold Noodle Salad)

Home-Style Chirashi Sushi

Sukiyaki

The bold paintings of fish on this 17th-century porcelain dish reflect the central role of fish in the Japanese diet. It is a staple in this mountainous island nation and is served, both raw and cooked, at virtually every meal. The fish on this plate resemble sea bass, a fish often served as the delicacy *sashimi*.

According to Japanese myth, when the god Izanagi came to earth, he dropped his necklace, which became the very first chrysanthemum. The flower has been part of Japanese tradition for centuries, serving as the emblem for the royal family for almost a thousand years. This porcelain bowl from the late 17th or early 18th century takes the form of a chrysanthemum and features painted floral decorations, as well as the image of a phoenix. Some varieties of the flower provide Japanese cooks with greens for salads.

MISO-SHIRU
(Miso Soup)

4 teaspoons miso* (fermented soybean paste; white, red, or a mixture)

4 cups dashi (fish broth; easily prepared by mixing Hondashi* and water according to instructions)

2 ounces wakame* seaweed, dried and cut

4 ounces soft tofu, drained and cut into ¼-inch cubes

1 scallion, diced

*Available in Asian groceries and specialty stores.

In a medium saucepan, stir the miso and 1 cup of the *dashi* together. When the miso has dissolved, add the *wakame,* tofu, and remaining *dashi* and place over medium heat. Bring to a boil, reduce heat, and simmer until the tofu begins to float on the surface. Remove from heat immediately. Adjust seasonings to taste by adding extra miso or *dashi.* To serve, ladle into individual bowls and garnish with scallions. *Serves 4.*

SPINACH GOMA-AE
(Spinach Salad with Sesame-Seed Dressing)

1 pound fresh spinach, well-rinsed, with stems removed

½ cup sesame seeds, roasted in a 350°F oven until golden brown (5 to 10 minutes)

½ cup sugar

¼ cup soy sauce

¼ cup mirin* (sweet cooking wine) or sake*

*Available in Asian groceries and specialty stores.

Bring a large pot of lightly salted water to a boil. Fill another large bowl with ice water. Put the spinach in the boiling water and cook for about 1 minute, until the spinach is limp but still bright green. Remove the spinach and immediately immerse it in the ice water to cool. Drain the spinach and gently squeeze out any remaining water. Chop the spinach coarsely and divide it among four small bowls.

To prepare the dressing, place the remaining ingredients in a blender or food processor and process until the mixture forms a smooth paste.

To serve, top each bowl of spinach with about 2 tablespoons of the dressing. *Serves 4.*

AGE DASHI-TOFU
(Deep-Fried Tofu with Tempura Sauce)

TEMPURA SAUCE:

1 cup dashi *(fish broth; easily prepared by
  mixing* Hondashi * and water according
  to instructions)*

¹/₄ cup soy sauce

¹/₄ cup mirin* *(sweet cooking wine)
  or 1 cup* sake *plus 1 teaspoon sugar*

vegetable oil for deep-frying

1 cake (12 ounces) firm tofu

1 tablespoon flour

GARNISH:

daikon radish, grated

hana-katsuo* *(dried shaved bonito
  {a type of mackerel})*

1 scallion, finely chopped

**Available in Asian groceries and
  specialty stores.*

Combine all the sauce ingredients in a small saucepan and bring to a boil.
Immediately remove from heat.

Using a deep-fry thermometer, heat the vegetable oil to 350°F in a heavy frying
pan or wok. Drain the tofu and remove excess water by squeezing gently with paper
towels. Cut the tofu into 1-inch cubes and gently toss with the flour. Carefully place
the tofu cubes in the hot oil and fry until lightly browned and crispy, about 5 to 7
minutes. Remove and drain on paper towels.

To serve, arrange the fried tofu cubes in a bowl and pour the hot tempura sauce
over them. Garnish with the grated radish, *hana-katsuo,* and scallions. *Serves 4 as an
appetizer.*

The term *ukiyo-e* ("pictures of the floating world") originally
referred to the Buddhist concept of the transitory nature of
life. In time the woodblock prints known as *ukiyo-e* came
to celebrate life's ephemeral pleasures, especially the more
glamorous and expensive ones. The audience for *ukiyo-e*
prints enjoyed seeing the exploits of wealthy and famous
people, to whom the rules of a rigid society did not seem
to apply.

In this print by **Torii Kiyonaga** from the early 1780s,
a wealthy man in a black kimono (at right) begins a summer
evening's entertainment among the geishas in the pleasure
district of his town. As a woman serenades him on a stringed
instrument called a *samisen,* one of the men on the left
offers the gentleman a cup of *sake.* A Japanese wine made
from rice, sake was rarely served at meals, being reserved
for religious libations or festive occasions such as the one
shown here.

While it had its roots in Zen Buddhism, the Japanese tea ceremony was reflected constantly in daily life. For example, in the 1770s the phrase "flying tea-ceremony kettle" had come to be slang for an attractive woman. **Ippitsusai Bunchō**'s print plays on this meaning, presenting an alluring woman making tea while the ceremonial kettle sprouts wings and takes flight. This scene is set in winter, a season during which the beverage was made over an open hearth inside the house.

TEBA-KARAAGE
(Fried Chicken Wings)

---

vegetable oil for deep-frying
*8 chicken wings, wing tips removed, cut in
    half at joint*
½ teaspoon salt

2 tablespoons soy sauce
dash of sesame oil
2 tablespoons flour

Using a deep-fry thermometer, heat the oil to 350°F in a wok or large, heavy pot. Rinse the wings under cold water and pat dry with paper towels. Mix the remaining ingredients together. Toss the wings in the flour mixture. Carefully place the wings in the hot oil and fry until dark and crispy, about 5 minutes. Remove the wings from the oil and drain on paper towels. Serve hot. *Serves 4 as an appetizer.*

YAKISOBA
(Stir-Fried Noodles)

---

2 tablespoons vegetable oil
¼ pound ground beef, pork, chicken, or sausage
*¼ head cabbage, cored and shredded into
    2-inch lengths*
10 mushrooms, thinly sliced
10 pea pods, julienned

1 pound yakisoba* *noodles or 4 packages
    ramen noodles, cooked according to instruc-
    tions and drained*
½ cup tonkatsu* *sauce*

**Available in Asian groceries and
specialty stores.*

Heat the oil over high heat in a wok or large skillet. Add the ground meat and stir-fry, breaking up lumps, until it loses its pink color. Drain any excess oil from the pan and add the vegetables. Stir-fry until the cabbage is tender, about 2 minutes. Add the noodles and *tonkatsu* sauce. Continue stir-frying and separating the noodles until the noodles absorb the sauce, about 3 minutes. Taste and add more sauce if desired. Serve immediately. *Serves 4.*

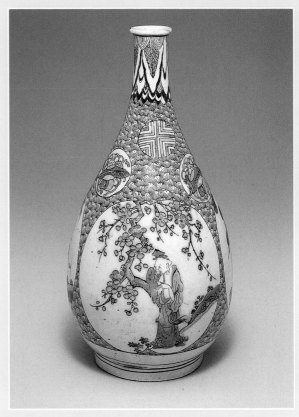

This 17th-century Japanese bottle not only is shaped like a pear, but features a painting of a pear tree, beneath which sits a Chinese sage. A part of the Japanese diet since the 9th century, the Japanese pear, or *nashi*, is light yellow to brown in color and is like an apple in size and crispness. This tart, juicy fruit often follows Japanese meals as a dessert.

By the late 1700s, the population of Edo (present-day Tokyo) had grown to about 1 million, making it the largest city in Japan and one of the most populous in the world. An especially lively section of the city lay along the Sumida River, where pleasure boats and river parties were common and whose banks were lined with fashionable restaurants and teahouses.

Tea was central to the Japanese not only in the private realm of the tea ceremony, but in the public sphere as well. In the bustling urban centers of 18th-century Japan, teahouses served a role similar to the one played by cafés in Europe in the next century as places for discussion, socializing, and entertainment. This print by **Angyusai Enshi**, *View from the Balcony of the Yamashiro Teahouse*, c. 1792, is a triptych, of which two panels are shown here.

HIYASHI-CHUKA SOBA
(Cold Noodle Salad)

DRESSING:

¹/₂ cup dashi (fish broth; easily prepared by mixing Hondashi* and water according to instructions)

1 cup rice vinegar

²/₃ cup soy sauce

1 cup sugar

dash of sesame oil

SALAD:

4 packages ramen noodles, cooked according to instructions, drained and cooled

2 cups iceberg lettuce, julienned

1 tomato, sliced

1 cup bean sprouts, steamed briefly and cooled

1 cup broccoli pieces, steamed and cooled

1 cup cooked chicken, cooled and chopped

1 cup salad shrimp, cooked and cooled

1 egg, fried over-hard

2 teaspoons sesame seeds, roasted in a 350°F oven until golden brown (5 to 10 minutes)

¹/₂ cup gari* (pickled ginger) as a garnish

*Available in Asian groceries and specialty stores.

Blend the dressing ingredients together. (Dressing may be stored in the refrigerator for up to 3 weeks.) To serve, toss the noodles with ¼ cup of the dressing and divide among four plates. Arrange the vegetables, chicken, shrimp, and egg on top of the noodles and drizzle more dressing over the salads. Sprinkle with the sesame seeds and place a small amount of the *gari* on the side of each salad. *Serves 4.*

While most *ukiyo-e* prints celebrate the lives of the rich and famous, by the end of the 18th century, a new type of print appeared that portrayed more humble, realistic subjects. This rare print by **Rekisentie Eiri** from the 1790s portrays a waitress at the Izumi-ya Teahouse. From a rich mica background, she emerges to fill the frame in a bold composition that emphasizes her individuality. Her fan bears the portrait of a popular actor of the day, proving that *she* has not lost her interest in celebrities.

RESTAURANT ON THE PARK

The Art Institute of Chicago, 111 South Michigan Avenue, Chicago

---

Spinach Salad with Fresh Fennel, Roquefort Cheese, and Prosciutto

Bibb Lettuce and Radicchio with Marinated Asparagus and Gazpacho Dressing

Grilled Sea Scallops with Artichoke Hearts, Lemon-Herb Sauce, and Fried Leeks

Cold, Poached Chicken Breast Stuffed with Spinach and Goat Cheese

Roasted, Honey-Glazed Quail Stuffed with Duck Sausage and Wild Mushrooms

Pan-Roasted Lamb Chops with Grilled-Vegetable Ratatouille

Apple Tart with Caramel Sauce

Chocolate Mille-Feuille with Apricot Sauce

This massive, silver tureen was created in 1824 or 1825 by **John Bridge** for King George IV, who regularly commissioned silver pieces for state occasions. The tureen depicts Triton, son of Poseidon, the Greek god of the sea, sitting atop a giant clam shell supported by three hippocampi, the fish-tailed horses of mythology; the entire piece rests on the backs of six small silver turtles. An example of the revival of interest in the Rococo style in 19th-century England, this ornate tureen was the first of five nearly identical pieces produced by Bridge for the king.

SPINACH SALAD WITH FRESH FENNEL, ROQUEFORT CHEESE, AND PROSCIUTTO

1 pound spinach, washed, with stems removed
1/2 head radicchio, shredded
1 fennel bulb, thinly sliced
4 ounces prosciutto, julienned

DRESSING:
1 cup olive oil

1/2 cup extra-virgin olive oil
1/2 cup sherry vinegar
salt and pepper to taste

4 cherry tomatoes, halved
4 ounces Roquefort cheese, crumbled

Mix the spinach and radicchio in a large bowl. Add the fennel and prosciutto and toss. Combine the oil and vinegar and mix thoroughly; add salt and pepper to taste. Toss the salad with the dressing. Spoon into chilled bowls, top with the tomato halves and cheese, and serve. *Serves 4.*

BIBB LETTUCE AND RADICCHIO WITH MARINATED ASPARAGUS AND GAZPACHO DRESSING

GAZPACHO DRESSING:

2½ cups olive oil

1 cup red-wine vinegar

½ cup tomato juice

2 garlic cloves, minced

salt and freshly ground pepper to taste

1 seedless cucumber, peeled and diced into
⅛-inch cubes

2 medium tomatoes, peeled, seeds removed and
diced into ⅛-inch cubes

1 green bell pepper, diced into ⅛-inch cubes

1 yellow bell pepper, diced into ⅛-inch cubes

2 stalks celery, diced into ⅛-inch cubes

½ red onion, diced into ⅛-inch cubes

16 asparagus spears, each trimmed to a length
of 4 inches

1 cup olive oil

½ cup red wine vinegar

2 heads bibb lettuce, washed, leaves separated

1 head radicchio, washed, leaves separated

2 plum tomatoes, sliced

Bring a large pot of lightly salted water to a boil. While the water is heating, prepare the dressing. Blend the oil, vinegar, tomato juice, garlic, salt, and pepper. Add the vegetables and mix. Set aside.

Blanch the asparagus in the boiling water for about 2 minutes, then remove and immerse in a bowl of ice water until cool. Mix the oil and vinegar together and coat the asparagus with the mixture.

Place the lettuce leaves on a chilled plate. Top with the radicchio leaves and sliced tomatoes. Fan the asparagus on top of the greens and spoon the dressing evenly onto the salad. Serve with freshly ground pepper. *Serves 4 as an appetizer.*

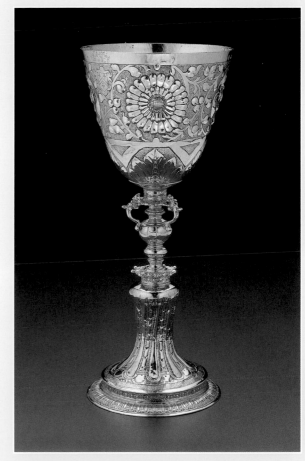

An Englishman named Hugh Redyke owned this silver standing cup of 1607–1608. The cup features bold designs of sunflowers and roses. The latter are not merely benign decorations but symbols of the Tudors, the royal family whose reign had just ended with the death of Elizabeth I in 1603. Usually intended for display rather than drinking, cups such as this one were so highly prized in 17th-century England that they were often mentioned in wills.

GRILLED SEA SCALLOPS WITH ARTICHOKE HEARTS, LEMON-HERB SAUCE, AND FRIED LEEKS

The dark vision of Chicago artist **Ivan Albright** is well represented in the Art Institute's collection. His unblinking, minutely detailed portrayals of aging and decay may have had their genesis in Albright's experiences as a medical illustrator during World War I. The subjects of *Plattered Fish, Georgia, 1966*—one of his occasional still lifes—may at first seem rather repellent, but, compared to his human subjects, are positively appetizing.

16 sea scallops, small side muscle removed
½ cup olive oil
2 tablespoons fresh basil, chopped
2 tablespoons fresh thyme, chopped
2 tablespoons fresh tarragon, chopped
1 tablespoon fresh rosemary, chopped

1 leek, washed and julienned
  (white portion only)
vegetable oil to cover leeks for deep-frying

1 cup white wine
2 shallots, finely minced
1 cup heavy cream
1 pound (4 sticks) unsalted butter, room
  temperature, cut into 1-inch pieces
juice of 1 lemon
salt and pepper to taste

16 small canned artichoke hearts

Place the scallops in a medium bowl. Mix the olive oil with half of the chopped herbs and pour over the scallops. Marinate at least 1 hour, covered and refrigerated.

Heat the oil to 350°F in a large, heavy-bottomed pot or wok on the stove top. Deep-fry the leeks until crispy and golden brown, about 1 minute. Drain thoroughly on paper towels.

Heat the wine and shallots in a medium saucepan over medium heat. Bring to a boil and reduce the liquid by half. Add the heavy cream and again reduce by half. Remove from heat and add all of the butter, one piece at a time, whisking until the sauce is completely emulsified. Add the lemon juice, remaining chopped herbs, salt, and pepper. Keep the sauce warm, but not hot, until serving.

Prepare the grill. Remove the scallops from the marinade and grill until just cooked, about 2 minutes per side. To serve, place four scallops and four artichoke hearts (unheated) on each warm plate. Top with the warm sauce and garnish with the fried leeks. *Serves 4 as an appetizer.*

COLD, POACHED CHICKEN BREAST
STUFFED WITH SPINACH
AND GOAT CHEESE

1 tablespoon vegetable oil
1 pound spinach, washed, with stems removed
1 teaspoon garlic, minced
4 boneless, skinless chicken breasts with fat trimmed
chicken stock (enough to cover stuffed chicken breasts—approximately 4 to 6 cups)
8 ounces goat cheese
salt and pepper to taste

SUN-DRIED TOMATO MAYONNAISE:
2 ounces sun-dried tomatoes (do not use oil-packed variety)
1 cup mayonnaise
2 tablespoons fresh basil, chopped
salt and pepper to taste

fresh chives, chopped, for garnish

Heat the oil in a sauté pan over high heat. Add the spinach and garlic and sauté until the spinach wilts. Set aside to cool.

Rinse the chicken breasts under cold water and pat dry. Lightly pound the chicken breasts with the flat side of a meat mallet. Place each breast top side down on a sheet of plastic wrap at least twice as large as the chicken breast.

Bring the chicken stock to a boil in a large pot, then lower heat to bring stock to a simmer.

When the spinach has cooled to room temperature, season each chicken breast with salt and pepper and cover with a thin layer of spinach. Crumble goat cheese over the spinach. Roll the chicken breasts into cylinders, wrap tightly in the plastic wrap, and twist the ends securely around the chicken.

Place the rolled and wrapped chicken breasts into the simmering stock. Poach until the internal temperature reaches 165°F, about 30 to 40 minutes. Carefully remove the chicken breasts from the stock, let cool a few minutes and refrigerate until serving. Do not remove plastic wrap.

While the chicken is chilling, prepare the sun-dried tomato mayonnaise. Place the sun-dried tomatoes in a large bowl. Pour 2 cups of hot water over the tomatoes and let them soak for about an hour. When the tomatoes have softened, remove four of them, julienne, and set aside. Purée the remaining tomatoes in a food processor. Mix them with the mayonnaise, basil, salt, and pepper.

To serve, spread the tomato mayonnaise on four plates. Unwrap the cold chicken breasts from the plastic. Slice each on a bias into four pieces. Arrange the chicken pieces on top of the mayonnaise and garnish with julienned sun-dried tomatoes and chopped chives. *Serves 4 as an appetizer.*

While the growth of restaurants and gourmandism in 19th-century Europe was an important culinary development, most people were left untouched by it. Cooking and eating remained a domestic act for the vast majority of people. Their frugal meals often featured the solid, affordable peasant foods that their grandparents had eaten. The Dutch painter **Evert Pieter** captured a simple repast in *A Family Meal.*

The British Arts and Crafts Movement was a response to the Industrial Revolution, specifically to the shoddy products and terrible conditions of factory work. It championed the value of handwork in the decorative arts and the value of such objects as artworks in their own right. In 1882 architect and designer Charles Robert Ashbee founded the **Guild of Handicrafts,** one of the most important Arts and Crafts workshops. The virtues of the guild are evident in this silver coffeepot of 1900/1901. The simple, hammered body, elegant border details, and richly finished surface all emphasize the hand of the maker, a silversmith now unknown to us, who worked at the guild.

ROASTED, HONEY-GLAZED QUAIL STUFFED WITH DUCK SAUSAGE AND WILD MUSHROOMS

3 tablespoons olive oil
1 teaspoon garlic, chopped
2 shallots, chopped
¼ pound porcini mushrooms, sliced
¼ pound shiitake mushrooms, sliced
¼ pound oyster mushrooms, sliced
½ pound duck sausage

4 cups whole wheat bread cubes, toasted
1 teaspoon sage
½ cup fresh parsley, finely chopped
½ cup chicken stock
salt and pepper to taste
8 semiboneless quail
1 cup honey

In a large skillet, heat the oil over medium heat. Sauté the garlic, shallots, and mushrooms until the mushrooms begin to release their liquid. Add the sausage and sauté, breaking up lumps, until it loses its raw color. Remove from heat and place mixture in a large bowl. Mix in the bread cubes, sage, and parsley. Gradually add the chicken stock to moisten the mixture. Season with salt and pepper and cool in the refrigerator.

Preheat the oven to 450°F. Stuff each quail with 3 to 4 ounces of the cooled stuffing. Place the quail on a rack in a roasting pan. Warm the honey until thin and brush onto the quail. Season with salt and pepper, then roast until nicely browned, about 10 to 12 minutes. Serve immediately. *Serves 4.*

PAN-ROASTED LAMB CHOPS WITH GRILLED-VEGETABLE RATATOUILLE

8 lamb chops, each 3 to 4 ounces

MARINADE:
2 tablespoons olive oil
½ cup fresh lemon juice
6 cloves garlic, chopped
2 tablespoons fresh rosemary, chopped

RATATOUILLE:
1 red bell pepper
1 ear fresh sweet corn
1 medium eggplant, sliced into ⅛-inch thick pieces

1 zucchini, sliced into ⅛-inch thick pieces
1 yellow squash, sliced into ⅛-inch thick pieces
1 tablespoon olive oil, plus extra for brushing vegetables and sautéing
½ cup tomato puree
1 teaspoon dried oregano
1 teaspoon dried basil
2 tablespoons pine nuts, toasted in a 350°F oven until golden, about 5 minutes
salt and pepper to taste
fresh rosemary sprigs for garnish

In 1881 **Pierre Auguste Renoir** traveled through Italy and the south of France (the Midi). That year he painted *Fruits from the Midi*, which shows produce common to the region: peppers, lemons, tangerines, tomatoes, eggplants, and pomegranates. While the artist probably chose these fruits more for their coloring and texture than for their flavors, we can imagine some of them appearing in that Provençal specialty, ratatouille.

Trim excess fat from the lamb chops and place them in a large bowl. Mix the marinade ingredients and pour over the lamb. Marinate for 2 hours, refrigerated.

Make the ratatouille. Prepare grill 15 minutes before using. Core the red pepper and remove the seeded membranes. Brush all vegetables with some of the olive oil. Grill the vegetables until lightly marked on all sides. Set aside to cool.

When cool, dice the vegetables into ⅛-inch cubes. Cut the corn from the ear. Combine the diced vegetables, the 1 tablespoon of olive oil, tomato puree, oregano, basil, pine nuts, salt, and pepper in a large skillet over medium-high heat. Cook the ratatouille, stirring occasionally, for about 5 minutes. Remove from heat.

Remove the lamb chops from the marinade and season with salt and pepper. In a large sauté pan, heat a small amount of the olive oil over high heat. When the oil is hot, sear the lamb chops on both sides, cooking each side for 3 to 5 minutes for medium-rare.

Spoon the ratatouille onto plates. Lay two lamb chops on each plate next to the ratatouille, garnish with rosemary sprigs, and serve. *Serves 4.*

Throughout history, the apple has had many mythological, biblical, and even scientific associations (remember the apple that struck Isaac Newton?—it really did happen). While the Pilgrims brought apple seeds and cuttings with them to North America, it was the efforts of John Chapman—a.k.a. Johnny Appleseed—that gave the apple its American flavor. Rather than scattering seeds willy-nilly, as he is often pictured doing, Chapman actually established nurseries of apple seedlings from Pennsylvania to Indiana from about 1700 to his death in 1745. **Charles Demuth**, a Pennsylvania native, painted the luminous watercolor *Still Life: Apples and Green Glass* in 1925. Combining elements of Cubism with his own style, it is one of the most masterful of Demuth's many still lifes.

APPLE TART
WITH CARAMEL SAUCE

ALMOND FILLING:
1/2 cup butter
1/2 cup sugar
1 cup almonds, chopped
1 egg
1 1/2 cups flour

1 sheet frozen puff pastry dough, thawed for 20 minutes
1 cup almond filling
2 Granny Smith apples, peeled, cut in half, cored, and thinly sliced

1/4 cup sugar
1/2 teaspoon cinnamon

APRICOT GLAZE:
4 ounces apricot jelly
2 tablespoons water

CARAMEL SAUCE:
1 1/4 cups sugar
1/2 cup water
1 cup whipping cream
2 tablespoons butter

Preheat the oven to 350°F. Make the almond filling. Cream the butter and sugar together with a mixer. Add the egg and mix. Add the flour and almonds and mix until blended.

On a lightly floured board, roll out the puff pastry sheet until it is stretched slightly in each direction. Cut four 4-inch circles from the dough and place on a cookie sheet. Place 2 tablespoons of the almond filling on each circle. Place the apple slices in a circle on top of each pastry circle, pressing the slices gently into the almond filling. Mix the sugar and cinnamon together and rub over the apple slices. Place the tarts in the oven and bake for 15 to 20 minutes.

While the tarts are baking, prepare the apricot glaze. Mix the apricot jelly and water together and bring to a boil in a small saucepan over medium heat. Remove from heat and set aside.

Prepare the caramel sauce. Place the sugar and water in a large saucepan and bring to a boil over high heat. Let mixture cook without stirring until it turns a medium caramel brown. Remove from the heat and slowly add the whipping cream and butter, stirring.

When the tarts are done, brush the hot apricot glaze over them. To serve, spoon the caramel sauce onto a plate, set a tart on top, and drizzle more caramel sauce over the tart. Serve warm. *Serves 4.*

John Sloan belonged to the group of artists known as "The Eight" which embraced the realistic depiction of life as it was actually lived in America's cities. In *Renganeschi's, Saturday Night*, 1912, Sloan captured the atmosphere of a popular, bustling Greenwich Village restaurant with which he seemed intimately familiar. He wrote of it: "The qualities of light and sense of the place as well as the life of the dining room [are] quite satisfactory. Painted from memory."

CHOCOLATE MILLE-FEUILLE
WITH APRICOT SAUCE

8 ounces bittersweet chocolate, chopped

APRICOT SAUCE:
6 ounces canned apricot halves, drained
6 ounces apricot preserves

CHOCOLATE MOUSSE:
8 ounces semisweet chocolate, chopped
2 cups whipping cream

$^1/_4$ cup cocoa powder
$^1/_2$ pint fresh raspberries or other fresh berries, such as blackberries for garnish

Place the bittersweet chocolate in a microwave-safe bowl or measuring cup. Microwave on high for 2 minutes. Remove, stir, and return to microwave, cooking 2 more minutes on medium. Remove and stir until smooth. Cover the back of a cookie sheet with plastic wrap. Spread the melted chocolate evenly over the plastic wrap. Place the cookie sheet in the refrigerator until the chocolate is set but still flexible, about 10 minutes. When the chocolate has set, carefully turn it out onto a cutting board and cut into 3-inch triangles. Return triangles to the refrigerator.

Prepare the apricot sauce. Purée the apricot halves and preserves in a food processor or blender until smooth. Chill the mixture for at least 1 hour.

Prepare the chocolate mousse. Melt the semisweet chocolate in the microwave following the instructions above. Then place the bowl of chocolate in a bowl of cold water to cool. Whip the cream until it holds stiff peaks. Pour the melted semisweet chocolate into a large bowl. Fold the whipped cream into the chocolate with a rubber spatula to make the mousse filling.

Fit a pastry bag with a medium star tip and fill the bag with the chocolate mousse. Take the chocolate triangles out of the refrigerator. Place a triangle on a plate and pipe the mousse over it. Place a second triangle on top of the mousse. Pipe more mousse over this triangle and place a third triangle on top. Repeat to make three more desserts. Chill until ready to serve.

To serve, put 2 to 3 tablespoons of apricot sauce on each of four dessert plates. Remove the chocolate triangles from the refrigerator and sprinkle with cocoa powder sifted through a fine sieve. Place on each of the plates and garnish with the raspberries. *Serves 4.*

Wayne Thiebaud's still lifes celebrate food as a modern American mass-produced commodity. He is interested in food that has been, in his words, "contrived and arranged to tempt us, to seduce us." Indeed, the sugary confections arrayed in a display window in *Cakes No. 1*, 1967, do tempt us, despite their uniform, impersonal appearance.

This 16th-century Netherlandish tumbler is made of green glass known as *Waldglas*, German for "forest glass." The name refers to the many glasshouses that were located near forests, where wood needed to fuel the glass-making process was plentiful. The knobby decorations on the tumbler, known as prunts, were made by applying drops of molten glass to the outside of the vessel. According to one contemporary source, such decorations had a practical purpose: to provide a firm grip for the "hands of drunken and clumsy people."

Chapter Four

ITALIAN

VA PENSIERO

1566 Oak Avenue, Evanston

Insalata San Francisco

Prosciutto di Parma with Warm, Caramelized Fruit

Italian Bread-and-Onion Soup

Sautéed Shrimp with Pistachio Pesto on a Risotto Cake

Potato Gnocchi with Pesto and Green Beans

Rosemary Fettucine with Grilled Artichokes and Pancetta

Roast Pork "Arista"

Strawberries with Balsamic Vinegar and Mascarpone Cream

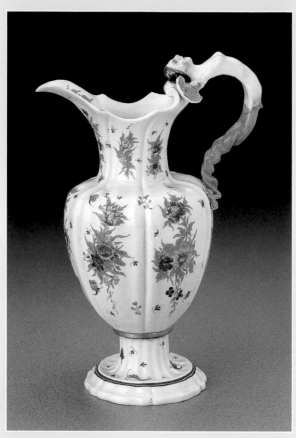

While the floral decorations on this porcelain ewer from the mid-18th century are in the style of the then-influential German Meissen factory, the shape of the vessel is based on a form popular in Italy during the Renaissance. The most surprising detail of this imaginative piece, however, is the sea nymph who arches her back to form a handle. The Italian taste for an eclectic mix of elements in porcelain wares is exemplified in this piece from the **Doccia Porcelain Factory** in Florence.

INSALATA SAN FRANCISCO

1 pound mussels or clams
½ pound medium squid, cleaned and
    cut into rings
½ pound uncooked small shrimp,
    peeled and deveined
4 medium sea scallops

juice of one lemon
¼ cup extra-virgin olive oil
1½ cups cooked white beans
1½ cups arugula leaves, washed
¼ cup fresh Italian parsley, chopped
salt and pepper to taste

Clean the mussels or clams and place in a medium saucepan. Add a small amount of water and steam open. Remove the cooked shellfish and discard the shells, saving the juice in the saucepan. Add 1½ cups water to the juice, place over medium heat, and bring to a boil. Add the shrimp, squid, and scallops. Cook just until the shrimp turns red and the scallops and squid become opaque. Drain immediately.

Whisk the lemon juice, olive oil, salt, and pepper together in a large bowl. Add the seafood, beans, and ½ cup of the arugula, and toss together.

Line a serving platter with the remaining arugula leaves. Pile the seafood-and-bean mixture on top. Sprinkle with the parsley and serve. *Serves 4 as an appetizer.*

PROSCIUTTO DI PARMA
WITH WARM, CARAMELIZED FRUIT

2½ tablespoons sugar
¾ teaspoon lemon juice
1½ ripe pears, peeled, cored, and cut into
    eighths, or 4 ripe figs, quartered

8 thin slices prosciutto di Parma,
    arranged on a serving platter
fresh mint sprigs for garnish

In a sauté pan, melt and caramelize the sugar over medium heat until it turns a deep golden brown. Remove the pan from the heat and add the lemon juice and fruit. Return the pan to medium heat and sauté, tossing gently, until the fruit is soft and cooked, about 3 to 4 minutes. Arrange the warm fruit over the prosciutto, garnish with mint sprigs, and serve. *Serves 4 as an appetizer.*

ITALIAN BREAD-AND-ONION SOUP

---

2 tablespoons olive oil
2 large Spanish onions, thinly sliced
5½ cups chicken stock
3 tablespoons dry Marsala wine or sherry

salt and pepper to taste
½ cup Italian bread, crusts removed and cubed
freshly grated imported Parmesan or imported Romano cheese for garnish

Heat the oil in a large, heavy-bottomed pot over high heat. Add the onions and sauté, stirring constantly, until translucent. Reduce heat to low and continue to sauté for approximately 30 minutes, stirring occasionally, until the onions are a rich, caramel brown.

Add the stock and bring to a boil. Lower heat and simmer for 30 minutes. Add the wine and season with salt and pepper to taste. Add the bread cubes and allow them to melt into the soup.

Garnish with the Parmesan or Romano cheese and serve. *Serves 4.*

This earthenware wine cistern, made in 1553, was filled with water to cool bottles of wine during banquets. Painting with permanent, transparent colors on ceramic pieces such as this required the same speed and precision as was required in the execution of contemporary frescoes. On the outside of this cistern, **Francesco Durantino** depicted a historical land battle, while on the inside he portrayed a marine scene from mythology—a clever conceit, given the purpose of the cistern.

The pear-shaped pilgrim bottle has its source in the dried gourds used by pilgrims in the Middle Ages to carry drinking water. It became a popular form for ceramics and metalwork in the 16th century. This example, in the tin-glazed earthenware known as maiolica, comes from Urbino in Italy and features grotesque designs over an unusual turquoise ground.

This scalloped bowl of blown glass from the 4th or 5th century could have held any number of Roman delicacies: ice cream, truffles, pepper from India, or flamingo tongues. Romans typically ate their meals lying on couches arranged in a U-shape. Dining rooms were called *triclinia*, meaning "three couches."

Earthenware, knob-handled dishes were often used as serving platters. The foods presented on such platters would have been seasoned with local herbs and spices such as coriander, fennel, garlic, parsley, sorrel, and mustard. This platter was made in the 4th century B.C. in a Greek city in southern Italy.

SAUTEED SHRIMP WITH PISTACHIO PESTO ON A RISOTTO CAKE

RISOTTO CAKES:
1 tablespoon unsalted butter
1 1/2 teaspoons olive oil
1/4 cup finely diced onion
1/2 cup Arborio rice*
1 3/4 cups chicken stock
salt and pepper to taste
flour for dusting
3 tablespoons olive oil

PISTACHIO PESTO:
3/4 cup unsalted pistachios, toasted in a 350°F oven for 6 minutes
juice of 1 lemon

1/2 cup fresh parsley, chopped
2 cloves garlic
1/3 cup olive oil
1/4 teaspoon cayenne pepper
1 teaspoon cumin
1/2 teaspoon salt

8 large or jumbo shrimp, peeled and deveined
2 tablespoons olive oil

*Available in Italian and Greek groceries and specialty stores.

Make the risotto cakes. In a heavy-bottomed, 2-quart saucepan, heat the butter and the 1 1/2 teaspoons of oil over medium heat and sauté the onion until translucent. Add the rice and sauté for 5 minutes.

Bring the chicken stock to a boil in a small saucepan, then reduce heat to a simmer. Slowly add the hot stock to the rice, 1/4 cup at a time, keeping heat low. Stir constantly until the liquid is absorbed, then add another 1/4 cup. Repeat, using all the stock. Season with the salt and pepper, then turn out onto a cookie sheet or flat pan to cool.

After it has cooled, divide the risotto into four equal portions. Form each portion into a flat cake, about 3 inches in diameter. Refrigerate until the cakes hold their shape.

When ready to serve, lightly dust each risotto cake with flour. Heat the 3 tablespoons of oil in a 9-inch sauté pan (preferably nonstick). Sauté the cakes on each side, turning carefully, until golden brown. Place the cakes on a cookie sheet and keep warm in a 250°F oven.

Make the Pistachio Pesto. Place the pesto ingredients in a food processor or blender and blend until smooth. (The pesto can be made up to 3 days in advance and refrigerated. Pesto also freezes well.)

Prepare the shrimp. Heat the 2 tablespoons of oil in a large sauté pan and sauté the shrimp in batches until they turn an opaque pink. Drain the excess oil and add 1/4 cup of the pistachio pesto. Toss thoroughly, making sure each shrimp is coated.

Place a warm risotto cake on each of four plates and place two shrimp on each cake, adding additional pesto if desired. *Serves 4 as an appetizer.*

POTATO GNOCCHI
WITH PESTO AND GREEN BEANS

GNOCCHI:

1 pound Idaho potatoes
1 pound large red potatoes
1 cup flour
3/4 cup grated Parmesan cheese
2 egg yolks
pinch of nutmeg
salt and pepper to taste

PESTO:

1 cup pine nuts
6 garlic cloves
3/4 cup olive oil
2 cups tightly packed basil leaves
1/2 cup Parmesan cheese, grated
salt and pepper to taste

*3/4 pound green beans, trimmed and steamed
until tender*

Preheat the oven to 400°F. Bake the potatoes until very tender, about 1 hour. Remove from oven and allow to cool for a few minutes. When they are cool enough to handle, peel the potatoes and press through a ricer. Set aside to cool completely.

Add the flour to the cooled potatoes and toss gently. Add the cheese and toss again. Add the egg yolks, nutmeg, salt, and pepper and mix to make a stiff dough. Roll the dough into long, thin logs and cut into 1-inch pieces. Roll the pieces into cylinders. (To make the classic gnocchi shape, mark the pieces by rolling with the tines of a fork and then pressing a crease along the length of each piece with the side of a fork.)

In a food processor, chop the pine nuts and garlic along with the olive oil. Add the basil and process until smooth. Stir in the cheese and add salt and pepper to taste. Set aside.

Poach the gnocchi in salted, boiling water, removing them as they rise to the surface. Toss with the pesto and steamed green beans and serve. *Serves 4.*

The secret of glassmaking was discovered somewhere in the Middle East around 2300 B.C. It was not until around 40 B.C., however, with the discovery of glassblowing, that a cheap and easy way of making glassware came to exist. Great quantities of glass flooded the market and became commonplace in Roman life.

This blown-glass jug from around the 2nd century would have held any of a variety of Roman wines. The most exotic were wormwood wine and rose-and-violet wine. Honeyed and spiced wines were often served from jugs such as this at the beginning of meals.

ROSEMARY FETTUCINE WITH GRILLED ARTICHOKES AND PANCETTA

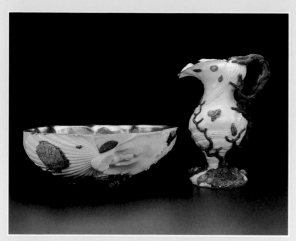

The 18th-century Rococo style emphasized imagination, novelty, and refinement. This ewer and basin—made of soft-paste porcelain around 1745 at the **Capodimonte Porcelain Manufactory** in Naples—is a masterpiece of Rococo design. The maritime motif is an appropriate one, given the function of these water-bearing vessels. From the coral handle to the pearlescent surface encrusted with shells, the motif is employed so creatively and consistently that finally the ewer and basin are as much sculptures as useful objects.

2 large artichokes
juice of 1 lemon
olive oil for grilling

ROSEMARY FETTUCINE:
2 cups all-purpose flour
3 tablespoons fresh rosemary, finely chopped
pinch of salt
3 large eggs
olive oil

6 ounces pancetta, diced (for best results, freeze the pancetta for 30 minutes, then dice)
1/2 cup water
3 cloves garlic, minced
2 tablespoons olive oil
4 plum tomatoes, peeled, seeded, and diced
1/2 cup chicken stock
salt and pepper to taste

Cut away the top two-thirds of each artichoke, remove the fuzzy choke, and cut off the remaining leaves. Peel the artichoke stem and trim the end. Bring a large pot of lightly salted water to a boil, add the lemon juice, and cook the artichoke bottoms until the stems are easily pierced with a knife. Remove the artichokes from water.

If you are using an outdoor grill, prepare it. When the coals are hot, brush the artichoke bottoms lightly with oil and grill until brown on all sides. (You may also broil the artichokes.) Cut each artichoke into sixteen wedges and set aside.

Make the rosemary fettucine. Combine the flour, rosemary, and salt in a mixing bowl and mix on low speed, adding the eggs one at a time. When it is thoroughly mixed, remove the dough and knead it on a board until smooth and elastic. Let the dough stand for 20 minutes. Roll the dough on the second thinnest setting of a pasta machine, following manufacturer's instructions. Cut the dough into fettucine (flat, wide noodles). Bring a large pot of salted water to a boil, add the pasta, and cook for 2 minutes. Drain and gently toss the pasta with a small amount of oil to coat.

In a medium sauté pan, place the pancetta in the water. Cook over high heat until the water evaporates, then stir constantly while the pancetta browns. When the pancetta is light brown, turn off the heat and remove the pancetta, leaving the remaining oil in the pan. Return the pan to medium heat, add the 2 tablespoons olive oil, and sauté the garlic until golden brown, but not burned. Immediately add the tomatoes, chicken stock, artichokes, and pancetta. Add the cooked fettucine and toss. Add salt and pepper to taste and serve. *Serves 4 to 6.*

ROAST PORK "ARISTA"

1 pork rib roast, 3 to 4 pounds, with chine
   bone removed (ask a butcher to do this
   for you)

STUFFING:

2 tablespoons olive oil
8 cloves garlic, minced
1 teaspoon salt
2 cups fennel fronds, blanched briefly in
   boiling water and chopped (if fennel is
   unavailable, you may substitute fresh dill,
   blanched and chopped)

MARINADE:

4 cloves garlic, minced
1½ tablespoons fresh rosemary, chopped
1 teaspoon fennel seeds
2 tablespoons olive oil
salt and pepper to taste

With a long, sharp knife, poke a hole lengthwise through the middle of the pork
roast for the stuffing.

Prepare the stuffing. Heat the oil in a sauté pan over medium-high heat and sauté
the garlic until just golden brown. Remove from heat and immediately add the
fennel fronds and salt. Mix well, then refrigerate.

Preheat the oven to 400°F. When the stuffing has cooled, spoon it into the hole in
the roast, making sure it is evenly distributed.

Combine the marinade ingredients and rub over the pork. Sprinkle with salt and
pepper. Place the roast on a rack in a heavy roasting pan, insert a meat thermometer,
and roast until the thermometer reaches 160°F, about 1 hour and 15 minutes. Let the
roast stand for 15 minutes before carving. *Serves 4 to 6.*

This earthenware *lebes*, or footed bowl with a lid, was
probably made by a Greek craftsman in Etruria in the
8th century B.C. Foods served in vessels similar to this
often included salt, a valuable seasoning and preservative.
Etruscans obtained the mineral from the salt marshes of
Ostia. Caravans carrying salt would travel from Ostia along
the Via Salaria, or salt road, to Etruria, stopping at a spot
along the Tiber River that over the next centuries grew into
the city of Rome.

Wine has been a part of religious sacrament at least since the time of the ancient Greeks, who believed that intoxication was a form of divine possession. In the Bible, wine and the vine are present both as simple facts of everyday life and potent spiritual symbols. In the Gospel of John can be found the story of Jesus and the marriage at Cana. When the wine ran out at the wedding feast, Jesus—with a little prodding from his mother—turned six jars of water into wine. This was the first of Jesus's miracles, which "made known the glory that was his, so that his disciples learned to believe in him."

    Giuseppe Maria Crespi painted his *Marriage at Cana* around 1686. It shows the decisive moment when Jesus performs the miracle. Here, as in most religious paintings of the day, a Biblical story has been transposed into a contemporary setting. The fine linens, silver and gold tableware, numerous servants, rich silk clothing, and classically inspired setting are representative of the fantasy and exoticism found in certain 17th-century Italian paintings.

STRAWBERRIES WITH BALSAMIC VINEGAR AND MASCARPONE CREAM

*2 pints strawberries, washed, hulled, and
  sliced in halves or, if large, quarters*
¹⁄₄ cup aged, imported balsamic vinegar
¹⁄₂ cup sugar

MASCARPONE CREAM:
2 pounds mascarpone cheese
8 egg yolks
²⁄₃ cup granulated sugar

mint leaves for garnish

Toss the strawberries, balsamic vinegar, and ¹⁄₂ cup sugar together and refrigerate. Make the mascarpone cream. Whisk the ingredients by hand or in an electric mixer until smooth.

Beginning with the mascarpone cream, alternately layer the cream with the strawberry mixture in a glass bowl. Cover and chill for at least 1 hour. Spoon parfait into individual glass bowls or goblets and garnish with mint leaves. Serve immediately. *Serves 4.*

In the ancient Greek world, water jars called *loutrophoroi* were used in the ritual cleaning that preceded wedding ceremonies. The scenes on this *loutrophorous*, which was produced in southern Italy around 365 B.C., show a bride preparing for her wedding with help from an entourage armed with mirrors, fans, jewelry, garlands, and oil. Most ancient ceremonies, such as weddings and funerals, included a meal.

PRAIRIE

The Hyatt on Printers Row, 500 South Dearborn Street, Chicago

---

Chippewa Wild-Rice Soup

Watercress-and-Cucumber Salad

Sweet Potato Skillet Cake

Prairie Eggs Benedict

Roasted Pork Tenderloin with Mustard, Buttermilk, and Rosemary

Lake Superior Whitefish Baked in a Bag with Onion, Garlic, and Herbs

Mushroom Crepes Stuffed with Duck, Rhubarb, and Leeks

Blueberry Angel-Food Upside-Down Cake

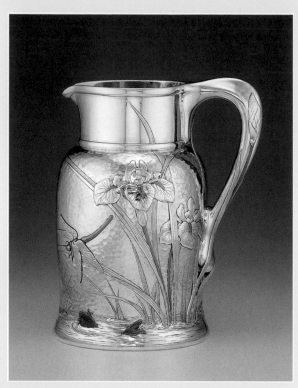

By 1878, the year this silver, gold, and copper pitcher was made, New York's **Tiffany & Co.** was well established as one of the world's leading suppliers of silver goods. Versions of this pitcher won acclaim at the 1878 Universal Exposition in Paris and found owners as far away as Russia. The pitcher's mix of highly finished surfaces and natural elements is characteristic of Tiffany's output at this time.

CHIPPEWA WILD-RICE SOUP

4 ounces bacon, finely minced
¹/₄ cup celery, finely diced
¹/₄ cup carrots, finely chopped
1 cup mushrooms, finely chopped
3 green onions, finely minced
1 cup cooked wild rice
2 cups beef stock

two 5.5-ounce cans V8 Juice
2 bay leaves
1 tablespoon fresh thyme leaves
¹/₂ tablespoon celery salt
dash of Worcestershire sauce
¹/₂ cup green peas, fresh or frozen
salt and pepper to taste

In a medium soup pot, sauté the bacon slowly over medium heat until it is brown and crispy and all the fat has been rendered. Add the celery, carrots, mushrooms, and green onions and sauté 2 to 3 minutes, until the vegetables begin to soften.

Add the wild rice and stir well to coat with the bacon fat. Add the beef stock, V8 Juice, and bay leaves and simmer slowly over medium heat for 20 to 25 minutes.

Add the thyme, celery salt, Worcestershire sauce, and peas. Taste the soup and adjust seasonings if necessary. Simmer for 10 more minutes, remove the bay leaves, and serve. *Serves 4 to 6.*

WATERCRESS-AND-CUCUMBER SALAD

DRESSING:
1¹/₂ teaspoons Dijon-style mustard
¹/₄ cup balsamic vinegar
¹/₄ cup corn oil
¹/₄ cup hazelnut oil
1 heaping tablespoon chives, finely minced
salt and pepper to taste

3 bunches watercress, washed thoroughly,
   with stems trimmed
1 pound cucumbers, scored and
   very thinly sliced
¹/₂ small red onion, very thinly sliced

Combine the mustard and vinegar in a medium mixing bowl and whisk well to combine. Beating vigorously with a fine wire whisk, slowly add the oils drop by drop to form an emulsion. Stir in the chives and season with salt and pepper.

Arrange the watercress on salad plates. Gently toss the cucumber and red onion in the vinaigrette, season to taste, and place on top of the watercress. Serve immediately. *Serves 4 to 6.*

SWEET POTATO SKILLET CAKE

2 egg yolks
1 cup heavy cream
¼ teaspoon nutmeg
¾ teaspoon salt
¼ teaspoon white pepper

1 medium sweet potato (12 to 14 ounces),
    peeled and sliced very thin on a mandoline
    or with a sharp knife
4 ounces Gouda cheese, freshly grated
3 green onions, finely minced

Preheat the oven to 350°F. Combine the egg yolks, cream, nutmeg, salt, and pepper. Whisk until well-blended and set aside.

Grease an 8½-inch ovenproof, nonstick skillet with a vegetable-oil spray. Pour 2 tablespoons of the egg mixture over the bottom of the pan. Lay several slices of sweet potato over the egg mixture to form a thin, even layer. Sprinkle 2 tablespoons of the cheese and 2 teaspoons of the onions over the sweet potatoes. Top with another 2 tablespoons of the egg mixture. Continue layering the ingredients in this manner, pressing them down occasionally to make sure all layers are covered with the egg mixture.

Transfer the skillet to the oven and bake until golden brown and firm to the touch, about 35 to 40 minutes. Remove the cake from the oven and let sit for 10 to 12 minutes. Run a knife around the sides of the cake to loosen it. Invert it onto a serving platter and serve immediately. *Serves 4 as a brunch entrée or 6 as a side dish.*

Taverns such as the one **William Sidney Mount** captured in *Walking the Line*, 1835, were among the few public eating-places operating in early 19th-century America. While the food served was rarely noteworthy, such inns were important places for meeting neighbors, sharing gossip, and drinking cider and whisky. Mount was sympathetic to the fact that gatherings such as the one pictured here were not accessible to all. He included a homeless man dancing for money in the center of the group and an African American standing to one side observing the revelry in which he cannot participate.

William Harnett was a master of trompe-l'oeil still lifes, paintings that "fool the eye" with their realistic detail. In *Just Dessert*, 1891, he assembled dessert foods popular in the late 19th century. Since American taste at that time was distinctly cosmopolitan, each of these delicacies is of foreign origin: coconut from the Caribbean, figs from Turkey, ginger from China in a ceramic jar, white Chasselas dessert grapes from France, and maraschino liqueur from Italy. Such extravagant items were more likely to be found in fashionable restaurants than in private kitchens. Many still-life paintings of food were hung in eating establishments and in private dining rooms in this period; this painting once hung in Dooner's Inn in Philadelphia.

In 19th-century Philadelphia, markets called "strawberry gardens" offered berries raised in nearby suburbs. These markets attracted fashionable Philadelphians, who delighted in snacking on the delectable fruit. The strawberries in this still life by **Raphaelle Peale** could have come from such a market. Peale belonged to America's most prominent artistic family of the early 1800s and has been called "the founder of the art of still life painting in America." The Chinese export porcelain featured in *Strawberries, Nuts, & c.*, 1822, indicates the intensity of international trade during the Federal period. The sugar bowl is decorated with an allegory of commerce and, by association, of prosperity.

New industrial processes in the 19th century brought more decorative arts to middle-class American tables than ever before. This coffee or tea service was made in the factory of **E. G. Webster and Son** in the early 1870s from sheets of tin alloy turned on a lathe; handles, spouts, and legs were soldered on, and the vessels were plated with silver in a chemical bath charged with electricity. One contemporary noted, "The enormous demand for articles of luxury, while very gratifying to the manufacturer, is another of the many evidences of the extravagance of our times."

ROASTED PORK TENDERLOIN WITH MUSTARD, BUTTERMILK, AND ROSEMARY

3 tablespoons Dijon-style mustard
1/3 cup buttermilk
2 pork tenderloins, 1 1/4 to 1 1/2 pounds total
1/2 cup parsley, finely chopped
3 tablespoons fresh rosemary, finely chopped
3/4 teaspoon garlic, minced
3 tablespoons vegetable oil

1 cup beef or veal stock
1 tablespoon cornstarch
1 tablespoon walnut oil
2 large cooking apples, peeled, cored, and thinly sliced
1 cup fresh cranberries

Make a marinade for the pork. Combine the mustard and buttermilk in a large bowl and whisk until smooth. Trim all visible fat and silver skin from the tenderloins and place them in the bowl with the marinade, making sure the meat is well-coated. Marinate for about 3 hours, covered and refrigerated.

Preheat the oven to 325°F. Combine the parsley, rosemary, and garlic, mix well, and spread on a plate. Remove the tenderloins from the marinade and dredge in the parsley mixture, making sure all sides are evenly coated. Reserve the remaining marinade.

Heat the vegetable oil in a medium nonstick, ovenproof skillet over high heat. Sauté the tenderloins for 3 to 4 minutes, turning frequently, until lightly browned on all sides. Transfer the skillet to the preheated oven and cook, turning once or twice, until done throughout but not dry, about 15 to 20 minutes depending on the thickness of the tenderloins.

Remove the meat from the pan and pour off any excess fat. Return the pan to the stove over low heat, pour in the beef or veal stock, and bring to a boil. Whisk the cornstarch into the reserved marinade and add it to the stock. Simmer slowly for 6 to 7 minutes, whisking constantly until slightly thick.

Heat the walnut oil in a medium sauté pan over medium-high heat. Add the apple slices and cranberries and sauté until the fruits soften, about 3 to 5 minutes.

Slice the pork and serve with the sauce and the apple-cranberry mixture. *Serves 4.*

At its root, Thanksgiving is a celebration of food and community. Among the dishes that may have been served at that first feast in 1621 are venison, roast duck, roast goose, clams, eels, succotash, wheat and corn breads, leeks, watercress, and wild plums. No turkey was reported.

Food is central in **Doris Lee**'s *Thanksgiving*, c. 1935, but more important is the sense of home, hearth, and family (though men are nowhere to be found in this bustling kitchen scene!). This painting, like many of Lee's, gives us a glimpse of an idyllic, rural American life that was fast disappearing in the Depression years from which this image dates.

Companions of Christopher Columbus discovered the pineapple in Guadeloupe in 1493. They were the first of many European explorers to enjoy what was to become one of the most popular American fruits in the world. While we associate the pineapple with Hawaii—which today produces three-quarters of the world's crop—the fruit was not introduced there until 1790. **Barnet Rubenstein**'s *Still Life with Pineapple, Grapes, Pears, Crabapples, and Strawberries* is from 1979.

New York silversmith **Cornelius Kierstede** fashioned this silver, two-handled, covered cup in the early 1700s. Such a cup would have probably been presented as a gift on such an occasion as a christening, at which it would have been filled with drinks such as syllabub, bishop, and caudle which were popular in colonial times. When inverted, the cup's cover becomes a saucer, with its three scrolled brackets serving as the feet.

LAKE SUPERIOR WHITEFISH BAKED IN A BAG WITH ONION, GARLIC, AND HERBS

2 tablespoons olive oil
1½ medium onions, very thinly sliced
2 medium cloves garlic, finely minced
four 6-ounce boneless Lake Superior whitefish fillets, with skin
salt and white pepper to taste
6 tablespoons mixed fresh herbs, chopped (such as thyme, tarragon, dill, cilantro, rosemary, chives, and parsley)
1 lemon, quartered

lemon butter sauce or 4 lemon wedges as an accompaniment

LEMON BUTTER SAUCE:
¼ cup dry white wine
juice of 1 lemon
3 to 4 whole black peppercorns
1 bay leaf
2 shallots, minced
dash of cider vinegar
¼ cup heavy cream
8 ounces (2 sticks) unsalted butter, cut into 1-inch cubes
salt and pepper to taste

Preheat the oven to 350°F. Heat the olive oil in a medium skillet over medium heat. Add the onions and sauté until they begin to soften, then reduce the heat and cook very slowly for 15 to 20 minutes until they are very brown. Remove the onions from the heat, drain well, cool, then mix with the garlic.

Place four small, brown-paper lunch bags on an ungreased baking sheet and spray the insides and outsides of the bags lightly with a nonstick vegetable-oil spray. Sprinkle the fillets with salt and white pepper. With the bags lying on their sides, place one fillet in each. Spread the onion-garlic mixture evenly over the tops of the fillets, then sprinkle with the chopped fresh herbs and juice squeezed from each lemon wedge. Close the bags tightly, securing them by piercing with toothpicks. Place the cookie sheet with the bags into the oven and cook for 18 to 20 minutes.

If desired, make the lemon butter sauce. Combine the white wine, lemon juice, peppercorns, bay leaf, shallots, and vinegar in a small sauce pot. Bring to a boil, lower heat, and simmer slowly until the liquid is reduced by half.

Add the cream, return to a boil, lower heat, and simmer again until reduced by half. Over low heat, slowly add the butter, piece by piece, whisking constantly until it is completely emulsified.

Season to taste with salt and pepper and strain through a fine-mesh sieve or cheesecloth. Serve immediately. *Makes about 1 cup.*

Serve the fish immediately with the bags still closed. Once diners have opened the sacks, the fillets should be removed and served with the lemon butter sauce or lemon wedges. *Serves 4.*

MUSHROOM CREPES STUFFED WITH DUCK, RHUBARB, AND LEEKS

MUSHROOM CREPES:
1 cup wild mushrooms, finely chopped
2 eggs
1 cup milk
¾ cup flour
salt and pepper to taste
1 to 2 teaspoons vegetable oil for frying

FILLING:
1 cup peeled and finely chopped rhubarb
⅓ cup sugar
2 tablespoons red currant jelly

2 tablespoons fresh thyme leaves
¼ cup red wine vinegar
1 cup ruby port wine
1 cup duck or veal stock
1 cup leeks, thinly sliced, blanched, and drained
salt and pepper to taste
1 tablespoon vegetable oil
½ pound boneless, skinless duck breasts

¼ cup cranberry relish as an accompaniment
fresh chervil for garnish

Beach plums, a species plentiful along the East Coast from Virginia to Maine, were among the first foods eaten by American colonists. Plums, in all their varieties, have remained a favorite on American tables. *Purple Plums* was painted in 1895 by **Cadurcis Plantagenet Ream**, a Chicago artist who produced many fruit-filled still lifes.

Sauté the mushrooms until soft, drain well, and set aside. When they are cool, whisk them together in a mixing bowl with the eggs and milk. Add the flour and whisk until a smooth batter forms. Season to taste with salt and pepper. Cover and refrigerate at least 1 hour.

Prepare the filling. In a medium saucepan, combine the rhubarb, sugar, jelly, thyme, vinegar, wine, and duck or veal stock. Whisk well and reduce over medium heat until thick and syrupy, about 15 to 20 minutes. Add the leeks and simmer until tender. Season to taste with salt and pepper, then strain through a medium-mesh sieve and reserve the resulting sauce separately.

In a medium skillet, heat 1 tablespoon vegetable oil over medium heat. Place the duck breasts in the pan and sauté 8 to 10 minutes per side until medium rare. Remove and let rest while you prepare the crepes.

Heat the 1 to 2 teaspoons vegetable oil in an 8-inch, nonstick skillet over medium heat. Remove the crepe batter from the refrigerator. Pour approximately ¼ cup of the batter into the skillet, tilting it so the batter thinly but evenly coats the bottom, pouring any excess back into the bowl. Cook the crepe slowly until well-browned, flip, and cook for another 15 to 20 seconds. Separate the finished crepes on wax paper. If the batter gets too thick, thin it with a little milk.

Slice the duck breast very thin with a sharp knife. Lay each crepe on a clean work surface and top with approximately 1 tablespoon of the reserved leek mixture. Place two or three duck slices on top of the leeks and carefully roll the crepe. Serve the crepes with the reserved sauce and cranberry relish. Garnish with sprigs of fresh chervil. *Makes 12 crepes. Serves 4.*

At the center of his stark *Movement No. 10, 1917,* **Marsden Hartley** placed the vital, rounded forms of fruits that glow with a warm color in contrast to the cooler tones of the hard-edged background. The two fruits in this still life, the pear and the banana, have long been popular on American tables. Pears have been an American favorite since colonial times, while bananas, imported from the tropics, gained popularity here in the mid-1800s.

Thomas Jefferson first introduced the eggplant to North America; this Asian fruit was one of the many non-native plants and vegetables he tried to raise at his Virginia home, Monticello. A century later, the most fashionable American restaurant of the day, Delmonico's in New York, was serving it—and claiming credit for introducing it anew. **Charles Demuth**, who made many studies of fruits and vegetables, including several of eggplants, executed this delicate watercolor of lush purple eggplants and plums in 1922 or 1923.

BLUEBERRY ANGEL-FOOD
UPSIDE-DOWN CAKE

1 pint fresh blueberries
2 tablespoons sugar

CAKE:*
³/₄ cup cake flour
1¹/₂ cups sugar
1¹/₂ cups large egg whites (10–12 large eggs), room temperature

1 teaspoon vanilla extract
1¹/₂ teaspoons cream of tartar
¹/₂ teaspoon salt
¹/₄ cup apricot preserves
vanilla or mixed-berry ice cream as an accompaniment

*You may substitute a prepared angel-food cake mix.

Preheat the oven to 375°F. Remove the top rack and move the other rack to the lowest position. Thoroughly wash your hands and all utensils before starting. (The cake will not rise with even a trace of grease, oil, or fat present.)

Rinse and pick over the berries very well and place them in the bottom of a plain, ungreased, 10-inch tube pan. Cover the outside of the pan with aluminum foil to prevent berry juice from dripping into the oven. Sprinkle the 2 tablespoons sugar over the berries and bake for 15 to 20 minutes until the berries release their juices. Remove from the oven and let cool to room temperature on a rack.

Make the cake batter. Sift the cake flour and ¹/₂ cup of the sugar together and set aside. Combine the egg whites and vanilla in the bowl of an electric mixer and blend at a low speed for approximately 1 minute. Add the cream of tartar and salt and beat at a high speed while very slowly adding the remaining 1 cup sugar in a steady, even stream. Continue beating until stiff peaks form. (To test for stiff peaks, run a rubber spatula through the whites. This should leave a trench that holds its shape. Do not over-beat whites or they will become dry and separated.) Remove the whites from the mixer and gently fold in the reserved cake flour/sugar mixture.

Pour the cake batter over the berries into the tube pan. Gently shake the pan back and forth to settle the batter and smooth the top using a rubber spatula.

Immediately place the cake in the oven and bake until the crust is golden brown and firm to the touch, about 35 to 40 minutes. (The cake may appear cracked or slightly shrunken.)

Let the cake cool completely on a rack for approximately 1¹/₂ hours. Loosen the edges with a knife or spatula and invert the cake onto a serving plate. Melt the apricot preserves in a saucepan over low heat and lightly brush over the berries to keep them moist and shiny. Serve with vanilla or mixed-berry ice cream. *Makes one 10-inch tube cake. Serves 10 to 12.*

Chapter Six

MEXICAN

FRONTERA GRILL

445 North Clark Street, Chicago

Enfrijoladas (Savory Bean-Sauced Tortillas with Fresh Cheese and Salsa Verde Cruda)

Cazuela de Hongos (Casserole of Woodland Mushrooms)

Codornices Asadas en Mole de Cacahuate (Wood-Grilled Quail in Spicy Peanut Mole)

Enchiladas de Jaiba (Shredded-Crab Enchiladas with Creamy Tomatillo Sauce)

Tortas de Papa a la Ranchera (Crusty Potato Cakes with Ranch-style Vegetable Stew)

Niño Envuelto de Chocolate (Chocolate-Mango Cake Roll with Prickly-Pear Sauce)

Born in Oaxaca in 1899, **Rufino Tamayo** was one of the foremost Mexican artists of the 20th century. As a young artist, he immersed himself in the archeological treasures of Mexico City's National Museum—an experience that shaped his vision of modern Mexican painting. While *The Fruit Vendor*, 1943, bears the unmistakable influence of Picasso and Cubism, it is thoroughly Mexican in its subject and in the warm, claylike colors Tamayo employed.

ENFRIJOLADAS
(Savory Bean-Sauced Tortillas with Fresh Cheese and Salsa Verde Cruda)

SALSA VERDE CRUDA
(Fresh *Tomatillo* Sauce):
5 or 6 medium fresh tomatillos*
  (about 8 ounces), husked and washed,
  or one 13-ounce can tomatillos, *drained*
hot green chiles to taste (roughly 2 chiles
  serranos or 1 chile jalapeño), stemmed*
5 to 6 sprigs fresh cilantro, finely chopped
½ small onion, finely chopped
salt to taste

Available in Mexican groceries and specialty stores.

3 cups cooked black beans
8 ounces chorizo* *sausage, removed from*
  its casing
⅓ cup vegetable oil
12 corn tortillas
¾ cup (about 3 ounces) crumbled Mexican
  queso fresco or similar fresh cheese such*
  as farmers or feta
⅓ cup thinly sliced onion
3 tablespoons fresh, flat-leaf parsley, very
  coarsely chopped

Make the salsa. If using fresh *tomatillos,* roast them under a preheated broiler until soft and blackened in spots, about 5 to 7 minutes. Canned *tomatillos* do not need to be cooked. Place the *tomatillos* in a blender or food processor and process to a coarse purée.

Finely chop the green chiles, removing the seeds if you want a milder sauce. Scrape the *tomatillo* purée into a sauce dish and stir in the chiles, cilantro, and onion. Thin to a medium consistency with about ¼ cup water, then season with salt. Let stand for about 30 minutes before serving, allowing the flavors to blend. *Makes about 1½ cups.*

Make the enfrijoladas. Purée the beans with some of their broth in a blender or food processor. Transfer to a medium saucepan, bring to a boil, and then lower heat to a simmer. Thin beans with a little bean broth or water until no thicker than medium-consistency bean soup. Season with salt if necessary. Let the beans return to a simmer, then cover and reduce heat to low.

In a small skillet, fry the *chorizo* in a little of the oil over medium-low heat, breaking up lumps, until all raw color is gone, about 10 minutes. Drain thoroughly on paper towels.

If the tortillas are moist, dry them in a single layer for a few minutes until a little leathery (this will keep them from absorbing much oil). Heat the remaining oil in a small skillet over medium-high heat. When the oil is hot enough to make the edge of a tortilla sizzle sharply, fry the tortillas one at a time for a few minutes on each side, just enough to make them supple. Drain well on paper towels.

Twenty minutes before serving, preheat the oven to 350°F. Pour out 1½ cups of the warm, soupy beans onto a deep plate. One by one, dip the tortillas into the beans, coating both sides. Fold the tortillas into quarters and lay them in two slightly over-lapping rows in a large, ovenproof baking dish.

Scrape any beans remaining on the plate back into the saucepan. If the beans have thickened beyond the consistency of soup, add a little more water or bean broth. Spoon the warm beans over the quartered tortillas, sprinkle with the *chorizo,* cover the baking dish with foil, and place in the oven just until the beans are bubbling, about 8 to 10 minutes.

When the *enfrijoladas* are heated through, uncover and sprinkle with the crumbled cheese, sliced onion, and chopped parsley. Serve immediately with the salsa. *Serves 4 to 6 as an appetizer or light entrée.*

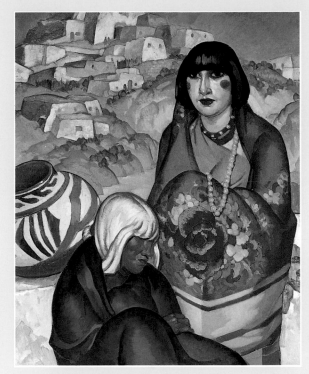

Along with Georgia O'Keeffe, Marsden Hartley, and John Marin, **William Penhallow Henderson** was one of a number of artists drawn to the land and culture of the American Southwest and Mexico. The Massachusetts-born Henderson made his home in Santa Fe; from there he traveled to document the Mexican-American folkways of the region in paintings such as *Ready for the Fiesta,* 1920.

Ancient peoples often signaled the importance of a food in their diet by making it a model for ceramic pieces. For the Nazca people of Peru, one of these foods was the achira root, a starchy tuber that they cultivated and that is still a staple in the region. Representations of plants such as this were tied to the agricultural ceremonies of the Nazca.

Dishes made from maize were staple foods of ancient American peoples. Whole maize kernels were soaked in lime juice to produce a thick drink to which honey or other flavorings could be added. And, of course, maize was the key ingredient in one of the most famous of ancient American foods, the tortilla. This *olla*, or storage vessel, was made around 1100 by the Anasazi culture in the southwestern United States. It was used to store meal ground from white, yellow, red, or blue maize.

CAZUELA DE HONGOS
(Casserole of Woodland Mushrooms)

5 ripe, medium plum tomatoes
  (about 10 to 12 ounces total)
1 large chile ancho* (dried chile poblano),
  stemmed and seeded
3 cloves garlic, roughly chopped
1 canned chile chipotle en adobo* (canned,
  smoked chile jalapeño in sauce)
½ teaspoon Mexican oregano*
1 tablespoon lard or vegetable oil
2 cups rich beef broth
1 pound mixed woodland mushrooms
  (shiitake, morel, oyster, lobster,
  chanterelle, etc.), cleaned, trimmed,
  and cut into thick slices

⅓ cup olive oil
3 large red onions (about 1½ pounds total),
  cut into thick rounds
½ cup chopped fresh epazote*
  (a light-green herb)
salt to taste
warm tortillas as an accompaniment

*Available in Mexican groceries and specialty stores.

Take care when handling chile peppers. Wear rubber gloves, never touch your face or eyes, and wash your hands thoroughly when done.

Preheat the broiler. Place the tomatoes on a baking sheet and set 4 inches below the broiler until blackened and blistered, about 5 to 7 minutes per side. Cool and peel.

Heat an ungreased skillet or griddle over medium heat. Tear the chile *ancho* into flat pieces, then toast on both sides in the hot pan, pressing flat with a metal spatula until the chile changes color slightly and blisters. Place the toasted chile in a bowl, cover it with boiling water, weight it down with a plate, soak for 30 minutes, then drain. Combine the tomatoes, chile *ancho*, garlic, chile *chipotle,* and oregano in a blender or food processor. Blend until smooth, then strain through a medium-mesh sieve.

Heat the 1 tablespoon of lard or oil in a large, deep skillet or earthenware casserole dish (*cazuela*) over medium-high heat. Add the strained sauce and boil quickly, stirring constantly, until reduced and thick, about 3 to 5 minutes. Add the broth, increase the heat, and bring to a boil. Reduce heat and simmer 30 minutes.

Prepare the grill (let charcoal burn down to medium-hot). Toss the mushrooms with half of the ⅓ cup of oil. Grill in a single layer until slightly softened. Coat the onions with the remaining oil and grill until slightly softened. (You may also sauté the mushrooms and onions over medium-high heat in a pan on the stove top in small batches until slightly softened.)

Break the onions into rings. Add the mushrooms, onions, and *epazote* to the sauce and simmer about 10 minutes to blend the flavors. Season with salt to taste. Serve with warm tortillas. *Serves 4.*

CODORNICES ASADAS EN MOLE DE CACAHUATE
(Wood-Grilled Quail in Spicy Peanut Mole)

SPICY PEANUT MOLE SAUCE:

2 *dried chiles* anchos* *(dried chiles* poblanos), stemmed and seeded

2$\frac{1}{2}$ *tablespoons lard or vegetable oil*

$\frac{1}{2}$ *small onion, sliced*

2 *cloves garlic, peeled*

1 *cup peanuts, toasted*

2 *slices firm white bread*

2 *canned chiles* chipotles en adobo* *(canned, smoked chiles jalapeños in sauce), seeded*

7$\frac{1}{2}$ *ounces canned tomatoes, drained*

4 *allspice berries or about* $\frac{1}{8}$ *teaspoon ground allspice*

$\frac{1}{2}$ *cinnamon stick or about* 1$\frac{1}{2}$ *teaspoons ground cinnamon*

3$\frac{1}{2}$ *cups poultry broth*

1 *tablespoon vinegar*

$\frac{1}{2}$ *cup red wine*

2 *bay leaves*

1 *tablespoon sugar (or slightly more to taste)*

salt to taste

8 *partially boned quail*

2 *tablespoons olive oil*

salt and freshly ground black pepper to taste

sprigs of fresh parsley and toasted peanuts for garnish

*Available in Mexican groceries and specialty stores.

Take care when handling chile peppers. Wear rubber gloves, never touch your face or eyes, and wash your hands thoroughly when done.

Make the mole sauce. Heat an ungreased skillet over medium heat. Tear the chiles *anchos* into flat pieces, then toast on both sides in the hot pan, pressing flat with a metal spatula until the chiles blister. Place the toasted chiles in a bowl, cover with boiling water, weight them down with a plate, soak for 30 minutes, then drain.

Heat 1 tablespoon of the lard or oil in a medium skillet over medium heat. Add the onion and garlic and fry until well-browned. Scrape into a blender and add the peanuts, bread, chiles *chipotles*, drained tomatoes, and drained chiles *anchos*. Pulverize the allspice and cinnamon in a spice grinder and add to the blender along with 1$\frac{1}{2}$ cups of the broth. Blend to a purée, then strain through a medium-mesh sieve.

Heat the remaining lard or oil in a large saucepan over medium-high heat. When hot enough to make a drop of the purée sizzle sharply, add it all at once. Stir for several minutes as the mixture thickens and darkens. Add the remaining broth, vinegar, wine, and bay leaves. Cover partially and simmer over medium-low heat for about 45 minutes. Remove the bay leaves. Taste and season with salt and sugar.

Prepare the grill, letting coals burn until medium hot. Cut the quail down the back, open out, and lay on a baking sheet. Brush with the olive oil, season with salt and pepper, flip, and repeat. Grill the quail, starting skin-side down, until just cooked through, 5 to 7 minutes per side. To serve, arrange two quail on each warm plate, spoon $\frac{1}{2}$ cup of sauce over each pair, then garnish with sprigs of parsley and peanuts. *Serves 4.*

This large, earthenware jar was made in the wealthy Mexican city of Puebla between 1700 and 1750. It features decorations inspired by the Chinese ceramics of the Ming dynasty that were imported by the Spanish to Mexico. One of the culinary specialties of Puebla is mole, a word from the language of the Aztecs meaning "sauce." Puebla moles are made from chile peppers; the most famous is made from red peppers and chocolate and is served on turkey and chicken.

"A better spice than our pepper" wrote Christopher Columbus of the American chili pepper after becoming the first European to taste one. With dozens of types varying in color from red to yellow to green and in flavor from mild to fiery, the chili pepper has been used in the Americas as both a seasoning and a food itself from as early as 7000 B.C. This Inca dish from the 15th or 16th century features two varieties of chili peppers and a type of fish, known as *suche*, that is exclusive to Lake Titicaca in the Andes of Peru.

ENCHILADAS DE JAIBA
(Shredded-Crab Enchiladas with Creamy Tomatillo *Sauce)*

CRAB:

1 tablespoon olive oil

1 small onion, peeled and diced

8 ounces fresh tomatillos,* *husked, washed and diced*

12 ounces cooked crab meat, carefully picked over and broken into large shreds

¹/₂ cup fresh cilantro, finely chopped

SAUCE:

1 pound fresh tomatillos,* *husked and washed*

2 or 3 chiles jalapeños, stemmed, seeded, and chopped

2 cloves garlic, peeled and chopped

1 tablespoon lard or vegetable oil

1 cup fish broth or light-flavored poultry broth

¹/₂ cup whipping cream

6 sprigs fresh cilantro, chopped

salt to taste

12 corn tortillas

¹/₂ cup Mexican queso añejo or similar aged cheese such as dry feta or mild Parmesan, finely crumbled*

several slices onion, broken into rings, and several sprigs fresh cilantro for garnish

**Available in Mexican groceries and specialty stores.*

Take care when handling chile peppers. Wear rubber gloves, never touch your face or eyes, and wash your hands thoroughly when done.

Prepare the crab. Heat the olive oil in a medium saucepan over medium heat, add the onions, and sauté until lightly browned, about 7 minutes. Add the diced *tomatillos* and cook for about 3 more minutes, until they begin to soften. Remove from heat, mix in the crab and cilantro, and set aside.

Prepare the sauce. Preheat the broiler. Place the whole *tomatillos* on a baking sheet set about 4 inches below the broiler and roast until soft and darkened in spots, about 5 minutes per side. Scrape the *tomatillos* and their juice into a blender or food processor. Add the chiles and garlic and blend to a smooth purée.

Heat the lard or vegetable oil in a medium saucepan over medium-high heat. When hot enough to make a drop of the purée sizzle, add the purée all at once. Stir for several minutes as the purée thickens and darkens, then stir in the broth and cream. Reduce heat to medium-low and simmer for 20 minutes. Remove from heat, stir in the chopped cilantro, season with salt, and set aside.

Line a vegetable steamer with a heavy kitchen towel. Place the tortillas in the steamer, cover, and set the steamer in a large pot filled with ¹/₂ inch of water. Bring the water to a boil, let boil 1 minute, then remove the pot from the heat and let stand 15 minutes.

(continued on page 76)

This Mexican sculpture from around 200 shows a village celebration complete with a conch-shell trumpeter, flutists, a drummer, dancers, children, and animals. It probably represents one of the great festivals of the agricultural cycle such as the harvest festival. Such celebrations would have featured the finest of foods: turkey, deer, and other game, maize, beans, chilies, squash, tortillas, and perhaps even dried fish brought inland from the coast.

In the sculpture, houses stand at the four corners of the village, and on top of them perch macaws, birds of special religious significance. This arrangement refers to the four corners of the universe, and was intended to symbolically align the festival and the life of the village with the spiritual geometry of the cosmos.

Squash was an essential food for the earliest inhabitants of Mexico, and was among the first foods cultivated there. This ceramic vessel from about 200 takes the form of a squash. Its legs are formed by macaws, birds prized by the ancient Mexicans for their colorful plumage and often used in rituals. Their appearance here indicates that the vessel was probably used in a religious ceremony. The vessel may have held a fermented drink made of maize or *pulque*, the juice of the agave cactus (this is the same juice from which tequila is made).

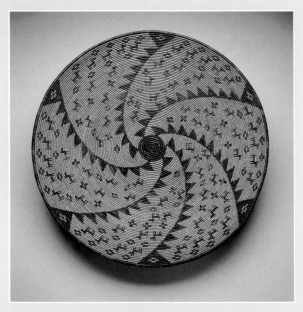

This woven Apache basket was used to winnow wild grains gathered on the plains of the American southwest. Such cereals were an essential part of the diet of hunting-and-gathering tribes. The familiarity these tribes developed with wild grasses and seeds through millennia of hunting and gathering led to the development of agriculture, which in turn led to the first sedentary cultures and, eventually, to the growth of great civilizations.

ENCHILADAS DE JAIBA *(continued from page 74)*

Preheat the oven to 400°F. Warm the sauce on the stove top. Mix a little warm sauce with the crab mixure and season with salt. Pour enough sauce into a 9 x 13-inch baking dish to cover the bottom. Lay a tortilla on a work surface, place a scant 2 tablespoons of the crab mixture in the center, roll up the tortilla, and transfer to the baking dish. Repeat, using the rest of the tortillas. Pour the remaining sauce over the enchiladas, being careful to cover the ends.

Cover the dish with foil and bake just long enough to heat through, about 5 minutes. Sprinkle with the cheese, garnish with onion and cilantro, and serve immediately. *Serves 4 to 6.*

TORTAS DE PAPA A LA RANCHERA
(Crusty Potato Cakes with Ranch-style Vegetable Stew)

POTATO CAKES:

2 pounds red-skinned potatoes, peeled

1 egg yolk

4 cloves garlic, peeled and minced

1/2 cup finely grated queso añejo* *or similar aged cheese such as mild Parmesan*

1 teaspoon dried thyme or 1 tablespoon fresh thyme

1 scant teaspoon salt

VEGETABLE STEW:

1 1/2 pounds plum tomatoes

1 tablespoon vegetable or olive oil

1 medium onion, sliced

2 cloves garlic, peeled and minced

2 cups poultry stock, vegetable stock, water, or tomato juice

1 large sprig fresh epazote* *(a light-green herb)*

salt to taste

1/3 cup flour

2 eggs beaten with 2 tablespoons milk and 1/2 teaspoon salt

1 cup dried bread crumbs

1/4 cup vegetable oil

1 cup sliced woodland mushrooms (morel, chanterelle, shiitake, oyster, etc.), washed and cut into 3/4-inch pieces

1 large chile poblano,* *blistered over an open flame or under a broiler, peeled, seeded, and sliced into strips*

2 large carrots, cut diagonally into thin ovals

1 cup green beans (about 2 1/2 ounces), ends snipped

sprigs of thyme, epazote* *(a light-green herb), or flat-leaf parsley for garnish*

*Available in Mexican groceries and specialty stores.

Take care when handling chile peppers. Wear rubber gloves, never touch your face or eyes, and wash your hands thoroughly when done.

Peel the potatoes, cover with salted water, and simmer until tender, about 20 to 30 minutes. Drain and cool the potatoes completely, then press through a potato ricer. Mix in the egg yolk, garlic, cheese, thyme, and salt. Form the mixture into eight cakes, ½ inch thick and 3 inches in diameter. Place the cakes in the freezer to chill.

Place the tomatoes on a baking sheet and set 4 inches below a preheated broiler. When blackened and blistered, 5 to 7 minutes, turn the tomatoes over and broil the other side. Cool, peel, and place the tomatoes in a blender or food processor along with any accumulated juices. Blend to a coarse purée.

Heat 1 tablespoon oil in a large saucepan over medium heat. Add the onion and cook, stirring frequently, until it begins to brown, 7 to 8 minutes. Add the garlic and cook 1 to 2 minutes more, then add the tomato purée and boil quickly, stirring, until quite thick, about 5 minutes. Add the broth, *epazote*, and salt. Bring to a boil, lower heat, and simmer, partially covered, for 30 minutes. Remove the *epazote*.

Remove the potato cakes from the freezer. Set up three plates, one with the flour, one with the egg mixture, and one with bread crumbs. One by one, dredge both sides of each cake in the flour, place in the egg mixture, flip over, then transfer to the bread crumbs. Flip once again and press the crumbs firmly around to coat all sides of each cake.

Shortly before serving, turn the oven on very low. In a large, heavy skillet, heat the ¼ cup oil over medium to medium-high heat. When it is hot, lay the potato cakes in the skillet in an uncrowded layer. Fry the cakes on one side until golden brown and crispy, then flip them over and do the same for the other side. Drain on paper towels, then place in the oven to keep warm.

Use water to thin the stew to a light, brothy consistency and bring to a simmer. Add the remaining vegetables and simmer over medium heat until all are tender, 8 to 10 minutes. Divide the vegetable mixture between four warm, deep dinner plates and top each with two cakes, slightly overlapping. Garnish with a big sprig of thyme, *epazote*, or parsley and serve at once. *Serves 4.*

In ancient Mexico, ideas about birth, death, growth, and harvest were often bound together. This funerary figure from around the turn of the 5th century accompanied a person on his or her passage from this world into the world of the ancestors. The ancestors lived in the earth and the mountains and acted as advocates for the living to the powers that controlled the rain and crops. Thus, a food such as maize, when placed in the bowl held by this figure, would have been an offering to the deceased, to the ancestors, and to the earth itself—all of which were believed to be linked in the cycle of cosmic regeneration.

Chocolate was considered the food of the gods in ancient Mexico and Guatemala. It was made by taking the seeds from cocoa pods, roasting them in an earthenware pot, and grinding them into a powder. The powder was mixed with boiling water, to which could be added chili, honey, or ground maize. Occasionally, participants in a religious ritual were allowed to enjoy this beverage. The Mayan *Vase of the Dancing Lords*, from the latter half of the 8th century, was used in this way; it shows the Maize God, the originator of human life whom chocolate-drinking Mayan lords emulated while enacting myths of creation.

NINO ENVUELTO DE CHOCOLATE

(Chocolate-Mango Cake Roll with Prickly-Pear Sauce)

MANGO CREAM:

1 package (1 scant tablespoon) gelatin

3 tablespoons orange liqueur
  (such as Gran Torres)

1/2 cup half-and-half

5 large egg yolks

2/3 cup sugar

1 2/3 cups ripe mango, diced

1 cup whipping cream

1 teaspoon vanilla extract

CAKE:

1 tablespoon butter

1/4 cup Dutch-process cocoa

3 tablespoons boiling water

3/4 teaspoon vanilla extract

5 large eggs

2/3 cup sugar, plus 1 tablespoon

1/3 cup cake flour

3 tablespoons Mexican chocolate* (such as
  Ibarra), finely chopped

PRICKLY-PEAR SAUCE:

3 cups prickly pears*, peeled, pureed, and
  strained (about 15 medium pears)

1/3 cup sugar (more as needed)

1 teaspoon orange liqueur

dash fresh-squeezed lime juice, if needed

powdered sugar for garnish

*Available in Mexican groceries and
specialty stores.

Prepare the mango cream. In a small, heat-resistant dish, combine the gelatin and orange liqueur and let stand for 5 minutes. Set the dish in a skillet of hot, but not simmering, water to melt the gelatin.

In a small saucepan, warm the half-and-half. In the top of a double boiler, beat the egg yolks and sugar with a whisk until they lighten a little in color and texture. Whisk in the half-and-half, set over barely simmering water, and cook, stirring occasionally, until the custard reaches about 180°F (it should lightly coat the back of a wooden spoon). Strain through a medium-mesh sieve, then stir in the liquefied gelatin. Place 2/3 cup of the diced mango in a food processor or blender and purée. Stir into the custard mixture.

Set the mixture over ice or in the refrigerator and stir regularly until it begins to thicken (it will look a little syrupy). Immediately whip the cream with the vanilla until it holds soft peaks. Gently and thoroughly fold the cream into the custard mixture, fold in the remaining mango, then cover and refrigerate.

Prepare the cake. Preheat the oven to 425°F. Butter a 12 x 17-inch jelly-roll pan, then line it with parchment paper, with the edges of the paper overlapping at the center of the pan. Butter the paper.

In a small dish, thoroughly blend the cocoa with the boiling water, then stir in the vanilla. With the whisk of an electric mixer, beat 3 eggs and 2 egg yolks (reserving the remaining egg whites) with the ⅔ cup sugar on medium-high speed until thick and light, about 5 minutes. Beat in the cocoa mixture. Remove the cocoa mixture from the mixer bowl and set aside.

Thoroughly wash the mixer bowl and whisk, then beat the two egg whites until nearly stiff. Beat in 1 tablespoon sugar and continue beating until the whites are stiff but still shiny. Sift half the flour over the top of the cocoa mixture and fold it with a large whisk or spatula. Fold in half the egg whites, then the remaining flour mixture, and finally the remaining egg whites. Immediately scoop the batter into the pan and gently spread it into an even layer. Evenly sprinkle with the chopped chocolate. Bake for 7 to 8 minutes until the cake feels springy. Remove from the oven, cool 3 to 4 minutes, run a knife around the edges, then lift out the parchment and cake together. Roll up the cake jelly-roll style, starting on one of the long ends, and peeling the parchment from the cake as you roll.

Prepare the prickly-pear sauce. In a medium saucepan, combine 2 cups of the prickly-pear purée with the ⅓ cup sugar, bring to a boil, then simmer until reduced by half. Cool, then combine with the remaining uncooked purée and orange liqueur. Season with lime juice and additional sugar, if needed. Cover and refrigerate.

Very carefully unroll the cake. Spread the now-set mango cream evenly over the cake, then roll it up again. Transfer the cake to a baking dish, cover with plastic wrap, and refrigerate until serving.

When ready to serve, trim off the two ends of the cake, cut the cake into 1-inch slices, and lay them, overlapping, on a serving platter. Sprinkle with the powdered sugar, spoon the prickly-pear sauce around the slices, and serve immediately. *Makes one 17-inch cake roll. Serves 12 to 15.*

Teotihuacan was one of the great political and religious centers of ancient America. Because Teotihuacan was located in a semiarid environment, its culture—from its government to its art—was dominated by deities associated with rain. This ceramic bowl features decorations in the form of a large figure with a feather headdress. It was used for religious offerings central to the life of this civilization.

Chapter Seven

GREEK

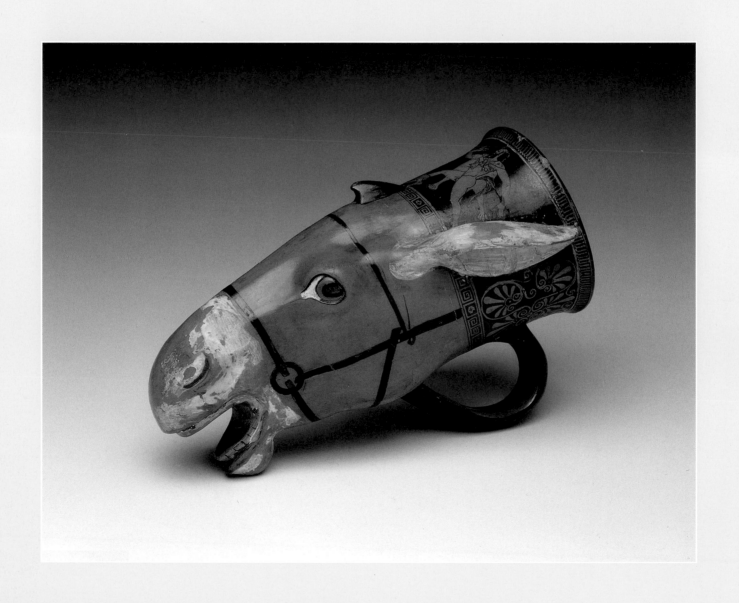

PAPAGUS
GREEK TAVERNA

Embassy Suites Hotel, 620 North State Street, Chicago

Olive-Bread Salad

Dolmades (Stuffed Grape Leaves)

Artichoke Pasta with Lemon-Cream Sauce

Chicken-and-Fennel Souvlaki

Roast Leg of Lamb with Eggplant Relish

Rice Pudding

Dried-Cherry and Pistachio Baklava

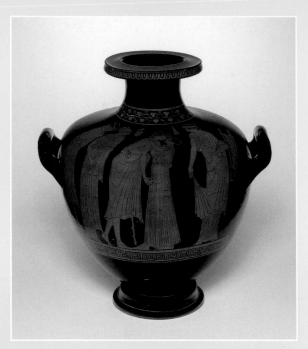

The Greeks of the 5th century B.C. drank their wine mixed with water. Slaves and women would fetch drinking water from public fountains and store it in three-handled jars called *hydriae*. The scene on this *hydria* features a man and woman embracing and sharing a kiss—an unusually intimate scene in the calm and elegant art of this period.

Pomegranates, fruits of many seeds, symbolize fertility in this gold necklace of the 6th century B.C. Pomegranate trees were easily grown in any Greek garden, providing fresh fruit and juice.

OLIVE-BREAD SALAD

SALAD:

½ pound olive bread;* cut into 1-inch cubes

¼ cup garlic-flavored olive oil

½ red bell pepper, seeded, grilled, and cut into 1-inch strips

½ yellow bell pepper, seeded, grilled, and cut into 1-inch strips

½ green bell pepper, seeded, grilled, and cut into 1-inch strips

2 heads frisée* greens, washed and leaves separated

16 small, black Kalamata olives*

VINAIGRETTE:

⅓ cup extra-virgin olive oil

2 tablespoons red-wine vinegar

1 small clove garlic, minced

¼ teaspoon cracked black pepper

⅛ teaspoon kosher salt

*Available in Greek groceries and specialty stores.

Preheat the oven to 300°F. Toss the bread cubes with the garlic-flavored olive oil. Spread the cubes in a single layer on a baking sheet and toast until golden brown and crisp, about 15 to 20 minutes. Cool completely.

Combine the bread with the remaining salad ingredients in a large bowl. Combine all the vinaigrette ingredients in a small bowl and mix well. Toss the salad with the vinaigrette until well-coated. Arrange on plates and serve. *Serves 4 as an appetizer.*

DOLMADES
(Stuffed Grape Leaves)

one 8-ounce jar preserved grape leaves
    or ¼ pound fresh grape leaves*
3 tablespoons olive oil
½ medium red onion, finely chopped
½ small yellow squash, cut into ½-inch cubes
½ small zucchini, cut into ½-inch cubes
¼ red bell pepper, cut into ½-inch cubes
½ cup long-grain rice
3¼ cups water, plus 3 tablespoons
¼ cup fresh dill, finely chopped

2 tablespoons fresh parsley, chopped
salt and pepper to taste
2 tablespoons pine nuts
juice of 1 lemon, strained
1 large egg white
plain yogurt and sliced lemons
    as an accompaniment

*Available in Greek groceries and
specialty stores.

Rinse grape leaves well in a colander. Fill a large pot with enough water to amply cover the grape leaves and bring to a boil. Boil the grape leaves for 3 to 5 minutes to soften. Drain well in a colander and let cool.

In a large, heavy skillet, heat 1 tablespoon of the oil over medium-high heat and sauté the vegetables until translucent, about 2 to 3 minutes. Add the rice and sauté until very light brown, about 3 to 5 minutes, stirring frequently with a wooden spoon. Add 1¼ cups of the water, the dill, parsley, salt, and pepper. Cover the skillet, reduce the heat, and simmer until the rice is tender but not soft, about 15 minutes, leaving the rice slightly undercooked. Remove from heat and stir in the pine nuts and half of the lemon juice. Allow the rice to cool slightly, then mix in the egg white.

Spread 2 tablespoons of the oil and the 3 tablespoons of water on the bottom of a heavy soup pot. Sort through the grape leaves and spread any ripped or otherwise damaged ones to cover the bottom of the pot. Snip any hard stems from the remaining leaves.

Make the dolmades. Spread a grape leaf out on a work surface. Place about 2 teaspoons of the rice filling at the center of the leaf. Fold the bottom of the leaf toward the center, repeating with the left and right edges. Roll to the top of the leaf to close. Place the dolmades seam-side down in the pot. Continue until all the filling is used.

Sprinkle the remaining lemon juice over the dolmades and add the 2 remaining cups of water to the pot. Place a heavy plate directly on top of the dolmades to keep them from opening, then cover the pot with a lid. Place over medium heat and bring the liquid to a boil. Reduce the heat and simmer for at least 1½ hours or until the grape leaves are tender. Serve warm or cold with plain yogurt and sliced lemons. *Serves 8 to 10 as an appetizer.*

Created as early as 2600 B.C. on the Cycladic islands of Greece, this figure may represent an ancient goddess of fertility. Fertility deities were central to many ancient peoples, who depended on healthy and plentiful crops for survival.

ARTICHOKE PASTA
WITH LEMON-CREAM SAUCE

This Greek *lekythos*, or oil bottle, was created in the 5th century B.C. At that time olive oil was not used only for cooking. It also served as lamp fuel and, when infused with flowers, as a cosmetic lotion.

10 baby artichokes, cleaned and halved (you may substitute 20 frozen artichoke hearts)
juice of 2 lemons

LEMON CREAM SAUCE:
2 cups whipping cream
zest of 1 lemon
1/2 teaspoon garlic, minced
pinch dry oregano
4 tablespoons plain yogurt
salt and white pepper to taste

1 pound Greek macaroni* (straw pasta), cooked al dente
2 cups fresh spinach, stemmed, washed thoroughly, and torn into large pieces
3 ounces feta cheese, crumbled
3 tablespoons bread crumbs
3 tablespoons grated kefalograviera* cheese (a hard, aged cheese, similar to Parmesan)

*Available in Greek groceries and specialty stores.

Bring a large pot of salted water to boil. Add the artichokes and lemon juice and cook until tender. Cool in ice water. (Frozen artichoke hearts will not need to be cooked at this stage.)

Prepare the lemon cream sauce. Place the cream, lemon zest, garlic, and oregano in a small, heavy-bottomed saucepan and bring to a boil over medium-high heat, stirring frequently. When the cream boils, remove from heat and set aside to cool 10 to 15 minutes. Add the yogurt, salt, and white pepper.

In a large sauté pan or heavy-bottomed pot, combine the sauce, artichokes, pasta, feta, and spinach. Toss gently and bring to a boil over medium-high heat, allowing cream to reduce slightly.

To serve, divide the pasta among four warm plates. Sprinkle the pasta with the bread crumbs and *kefalograviera* cheese. Place under a broiler until light brown, 30 to 45 seconds, and serve immediately. *Serves 4.*

According to Greek mythology, the wedding of Peleus and
Thetis was the setting of an event that led to the Trojan War.
Angry that she had not been invited to join the gods attend-
ing the wedding, Eris, goddess of discord and strife, rolled
a golden apple labeled "To the fairest" among the guests.
Picking it up, the embarrassed groom did not know whether
to present the apple to Aphrodite, Athena, or Hera. The
ensuing rivalry among the three goddesses led to the war.
In his painting *The Wedding of Peleus and Thetis*, 1636,
Flemish artist **Peter Paul Rubens** depicted the event as a feast
overrun by all-too-human jealousies and rivalries.

CHICKEN-AND-FENNEL
SOUVLAKI

Various depictions of Mediterranean fish and shellfish decorate this Greek plate from the 4th century B.C. These foods might have been served upon the plate; the well in the center would have held sauce or drippings.

Called a *lekanis*, this large dish from the 5th century B.C. was probably used to serve food at banquets, where such dishes as stuffed vine leaves and cheesecake might have been served. Recipes for various ancient Greek banquet dishes have come down to us through a Greek writer called Athenaeus, who wrote *The Learned Banquet*.

BLANCHING LIQUID:
2 cups extra-virgin olive oil
1 cup dry white wine
1/2 cup lemon juice
2 cups water
1/2 cup minced garlic
5 bay leaves

2 fennel bulbs, cleaned and cut into eighths
2 red bell peppers, seeded and cut into large wedges
2 pounds boneless, skinless chicken breasts, cut into 20 pieces

MARINADE:
1/4 cup red onion, finely minced
1 1/2 teaspoons dry oregano
1 tablespoon garlic, minced
1 tablespoon fresh parsley, finely chopped
2 small bay leaves, crushed
1 teaspoon cracked black pepper
2 tablespoons kosher salt
2 cups white wine
1 tablespoon lemon juice
1 cup extra-virgin olive oil

salt and black pepper to taste
3 cups cooked white rice

Place the blanching liquid ingredients in a large, heavy-bottomed pot, bring to a boil, lower heat, and simmer for 15 minutes. Add the fennel and blanch until slightly tender, 5 to 8 minutes. Let cool.

Assemble the souvlakis by alternating the chicken, red pepper, and fennel on four metal skewers. Place the souvlakis in a large baking dish. Combine all the marinade ingredients in a medium bowl, mix well, and pour over the souvlakis until well covered. Marinate, refrigerated, for 3 to 4 hours.

Prepare the grill. Remove the souvlakis from the refrigerator, reserving the marinade. Season the souvlakis with salt and black pepper. Place on the hot grill and cook, turning 2 or 3 times, until the chicken is cooked through and the vegetables are charred, about 15 to 20 minutes.

Meanwhile, place the reserved marinade in a small saucepan, bring to a boil, reduce heat, and simmer 10 minutes. Remove the souvlakis from the skewers, brush with a little of the hot marinade and serve atop cooked white rice. *Serves 4.*

ROAST LEG OF LAMB
WITH EGGPLANT RELISH

1 leg of lamb, boneless and tied, about
6 pounds
¹/₂ cup extra-virgin olive oil
1 sprig fresh rosemary, chopped
2 sprigs fresh oregano, chopped
2 sprigs fresh thyme, chopped
10 cloves garlic, peeled and chopped
salt and fresh ground pepper to taste

EGGPLANT RELISH:
1 medium eggplant, cut into ¹/₂-inch slices
1 medium red onion, cut into ¹/₂-inch slices
olive oil for grilling
salt and pepper to taste
2 ripe medium tomatoes, cut into 1-inch cubes
¹/₂ cup oil-packed, sun-dried tomatoes,
cut into 1-inch pieces
2 tablespoons fresh mint, chopped
¹/₂ cup extra-virgin olive oil
3 tablespoons balsamic vinegar

Remove any excess fat from the leg of lamb and place the lamb in a large dish. Mix the olive oil, rosemary, oregano, thyme, and garlic together in a small bowl and pour the mixture over the lamb. Marinate the lamb for at least 1 hour, refrigerated.

Preheat the oven to 400°F. Season the lamb with salt and pepper and place on a rack in a roasting pan. Roast the lamb until a meat thermometer inserted in the thickest part of the leg reads 140°F for medium rare, about 1 hour 15 minutes, or longer for a well-done roast.

While the lamb roasts, make the eggplant relish. Prepare the grill. Brush the eggplant and onion slices with olive oil to coat and season with salt and pepper. Grill, turning once, until cooked through and slightly charred. Let cool, then cut the eggplant and onion into 1-inch pieces. Toss the eggplant, onion, and remaining relish ingredients in a large bowl and keep at room temperature.

When the lamb is cooked to the desired doneness, remove from the oven and let rest about 30 minutes before carving. Serve the sliced leg of lamb on top of the eggplant relish. *Serves 6 to 8.*

This pitcher, or *oinochoe*, in the shape of a female head was made in Greece in the mid-5th century B.C. After wine and water were mixed in a large bowl, pitchers such as this one were used to pour the mixture into guests' drinking cups.

RICE PUDDING

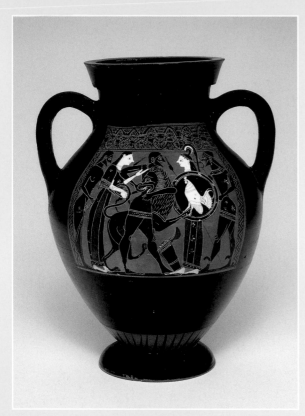

Amphorae, or storage jars, were often used in ancient Greece to hold wine. Greek wine was much heavier and richer than that of today. In addition to being served mixed with water, it was used in cooking to poach meats and in sauces for game. In the winter, it was heated and spiced to make a warming libation. The painting on this *amphora* shows Herakles fighting the Nemean lion, whose jaws he has pried open.

This elegant drinking cup from Greece, c. 480 B.C., is called a *kylix* and was used at parties and on special occasions. As the wine was consumed, an image of the goddess Artemis would appear at the bottom of the cup. She is striding through the night holding a burning torch to light her way.

¹/₃ cup Arborio* rice
1 cup heavy cream
1¹/₂ cups half-and-half
¹/₄ cup sugar
¹/₄ cup golden raisins
zest and juice of ¹/₂ orange
1-inch piece cinnamon stick

1-inch piece vanilla bean, split
1 large egg
1 tablespoon vanilla extract
1 tablespoon white rum

*Available in Greek and Italian groceries and specialty stores.

Soak the Arborio rice in a bowl under cold running water for 30 minutes. While the rice soaks, combine the cream, 1 cup of the half-and-half, sugar, raisins, orange zest and juice, cinnamon stick, and vanilla bean in a heavy-bottomed pot and slowly heat on low. Drain the rice and add it to the cream mixture. Keeping the heat low, stir the mixture constantly with a wooden spoon to prevent sticking. Continue cooking and stirring until the consistency is very thick and creamy and the rice is very tender, about 25 to 30 minutes.

Remove from heat. Discard the cinnamon stick and vanilla bean pieces, then stir in the egg, vanilla extract, and rum. Cool slightly, then add the remaining ¹/₂ cup of the half-and-half. Refrigerate at least 2 hours and serve cold. *Serves 4.*

DRIED-CHERRY AND PISTACHIO BAKLAVA

PASTRY:

6 sheets frozen phyllo* dough
½ stick butter, melted and cooled

FILLING:

¾ pound shelled pistachios, roughly chopped
6 ounces dried cherries, roughly chopped
¼ cup sugar
4 large egg yolks

SYRUP:

¾ cup sugar
¾ cup water
4 sprigs fresh mint
12 dried cherries, halved

*Available in Greek groceries and specialty stores.

Remove the phyllo dough from the freezer and thaw at room temperature for 2 hours. Preheat oven to 350°F. Combine the filling ingredients in a medium bowl and mix well.

To form the baklava, take three sheets of the phyllo dough, brush each sheet liberally with melted butter, and stack one on top of the other. Cut the stack in half, crosswise, to create two smaller rectangles. Spread each rectangle with filling, leaving a 1-inch border on all sides. Fold the long sides of the rectangles toward the center to hold in the filling. Roll it tightly like a jelly roll, beginning at the short side. Place the baklava on a baking sheet and brush with melted butter. Repeat to form four baklava. Bake the baklava until golden brown, about 18 to 20 minutes. Cool on a rack.

Prepare the syrup. Place the sugar and water in a small saucepan and bring to a boil. Add the mint and cherries and simmer until the cherries are tender, about 8 to 10 minutes. Lightly brush the baked baklava with the syrup.

Serve the baklava on plates with additional syrup spooned on top. *Serves 4.*

These small, glass bottles from the eastern Mediterranean were used to hold scented oils. Their shape copies popular clay jars of the day. At the time these bottles were made, around 300 B.C., glass was considered a luxury material for household objects.

Cornucopias, overflowing with fruits and vegetables, represent abundance and plenty. The symbol had its origin in the mythological goat's horn that was used to feed the baby Zeus. In mythology, the cornucopia was always full of whatever its owner wanted. This double cornucopia appears on a gold coin minted in Alexandria, Egypt, after 270 B.C.

Chapter Eight

GERMAN

THE BERGHOFF

17 West Adams Street, Chicago

Linsensuppe (Lentil Soup)

Kartoffelsalat mit Speck (German Potato Salad)

Pikanter Rotkohl (Sweet-and-Sour Red Cabbage)

Schlachtplatte (Sauerkraut with Sausages and Smoked Pork Chops)

Geschnetzeltes Kalbfleisch (Veal in Wine Sauce)

Hühnerschnitzel in Tomatensosse (Chicken Schnitzel with Tomato Sauce)

Apfeltorte (Apple Cake with Bourbon Sauce)

Alpenkuchen (Chocolate/White-Mousse Cake)

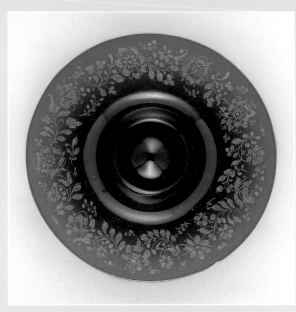

In the 16th century, glassmakers in Bohemia began to use diamonds to etch elaborate decorations onto plates such as this one and onto other wares. This technique had its origins in Venice, and Bohemian decorators probably used as models examples that had been carried from Venice through southern Germany.

LINSENSUPPE
(Lentil Soup)

1 cup brown lentils

3 cups cold water

3 slices lean bacon, minced

1 medium onion, finely diced

1 medium carrot, peeled and finely chopped

1 celery stalk, finely chopped

2 tablespoons flour

4 cups chicken stock

2 packets chicken bouillon granules

1 tablespoon tomato purée

salt and pepper to taste

¹/₄ pound smoked ham, cut in ¹/₈-inch cubes, and minced fresh parsley for garnish

Soak the lentils in the water overnight. The following day, preheat the oven to 325°F. Place the bacon in a Dutch oven or heavy soup pot with a lid and cook, stirring, over medium heat to render some of the fat. Do not brown. Add the vegetables to the pot and continue to cook, stirring, for about 5 minutes. Stir the flour into the mixture and cook 2 to 3 minutes more, stirring constantly.

Add the lentils, their soaking liquid, and all the remaining ingredients except the ham and parsley to the pot and bring to a boil. Cover the pot and place in the preheated oven. Cook for about 45 minutes or until the lentils are soft. Remove from the oven, season to taste, and serve garnished with the ham cubes and minced parsley. *Serves 4 to 6.*

KARTOFFELSALAT MIT SPECK
(German Potato Salad)

2 pounds small red potatoes, scrubbed
1 tablespoon salt

DRESSING:
4 slices lean bacon, cut into thin pieces
2 teaspoons flour
¹/₂ cup chicken stock
¹/₄ cup cider vinegar

2 teaspoons olive oil
1 tablespoon vegetable oil
1 tablespoon sugar
salt and pepper to taste

3 green onions (including some of green tops), thinly sliced, and 2 tablespoons fresh parsley, minced, for garnish

Place the potatoes and the 1 tablespoon salt into a large pot and fill with enough cold water to cover the potatoes by at least 2 inches. Bring the water to a boil and cook the potatoes until easily pierced with a fork but not falling apart.

When the potatoes are cooking, prepare the dressing. Fry the bacon, stirring, in a skillet over medium-high heat until crisp. Add flour and continue cooking and stirring for about 3 minutes. Add the rest of the dressing ingredients and cook the mixture, stirring constantly, until slightly thickened. Season to taste and set aside.

When the potatoes are done, drain and let sit until they are cool enough to handle. Peel the potatoes, and cut them into ¹/₈-inch-thick slices. Arrange the slices in a shallow casserole or dish in overlapping layers. Sprinkle the green onions and parsley over the potatoes.

Warm the dressing over medium heat. Spoon the warm dressing over the potatoes and serve. *Serves 4 to 6.*

Drinking was an important social ritual in late 16th- and early 17th-century Germany. Honored guests were expected to down the contents of a drinking vessel such as this 10-inch-tall Bohemian *Humpen* in one long draft. Despite its celebratory use, this particular vessel bears sobering enamel decorations illustrating the 10 ages of man, from the hoop-rolling child to the 40-year-old in the prime of life (symbolized by a lion) to the doddering old man led off by a skeletal embodiment of death.

Jutta Sika studied with famed designer Koloman Moser at Vienna's Applied Arts School in the first years of this century. In keeping with the goals of the Wiener Werkstätte, Moser encouraged his students to create designs to be mass-produced by the ceramics industry. Sika designed this playful coffee service for the Jösef Bock firm in 1901 or 1902. The bold, stenciled decoration was available in orange and green as well as blue.

PIKANTER ROTKOHL
(Sweet-and-Sour Red Cabbage)

---

4 tablespoons (¹/₂ stick) unsalted butter
1 pound red cabbage, cleaned, cored, and
*   shredded*
¹/₃ cup cider vinegar
¹/₂ cup chicken stock
¹/₃ cup sugar
salt and pepper to taste

ROUX:
1 tablespoon unsalted butter, softened
1 teaspoon flour

Preheat the oven to 325°F. Melt the butter in an ovenproof casserole over low heat. Add the cabbage and toss. Add the vinegar and stir together. Cover and simmer for about 5 minutes. Add the remaining ingredients except for the roux. Mix together and bring to a boil. Cover and cook over low heat until the cabbage wilts. Stir, cover, and place in the oven for about 1 hour. Stir occasionally.

To make the roux, mash the flour into the butter. When the cabbage is soft and cooked, move the casserole to the stovetop and stir in the roux. Simmer a few minutes over low heat until the flour can no longer be tasted. Taste, adjust seasoning, and serve. *Serves 4 to 6.*

SCHLACHTPLATTE
(Sauerkraut with Sausages and Smoked Pork Chops)

1½ pounds packaged sauerkraut
4 slices bacon, cut into small pieces
1 medium onion, minced
2 teaspoons flour
¼ cup chicken stock
¼ cup white wine
1 tablespoon sugar
½ teaspoon caraway seeds (optional)
1 tablespoon cider vinegar
salt and pepper to taste

1 bratwurst,* cut into 4 pieces
1 smoked thuringer,* cut into 4 pieces
1 knackwurst,* cut into 4 pieces
4 smoked pork chops,* fat trimmed

fresh parsley, minced, for garnish
boiled potatoes as an accompaniment

*Available in German delis and
specialty stores.

Preheat the oven to 325°F. Put the sauerkraut into a bowl of cold water. Wash, drain, and squeeze dry with your hands. Set aside.

Cook the bacon, stirring occasionally, over high heat in a medium pot until crisp. Spoon off all but 2 tablespoons of the fat. Add the minced onion and sauté a few minutes. Stir in the flour and cook another 1 to 2 minutes. Add the remaining ingredients except the meat, parsley, and potatoes. Add the rinsed sauerkraut and mix. Cover the pot and simmer over low heat for about 20 minutes, stirring occasionally.

Place a layer of the sauerkraut mixture in the bottom of an ovenproof casserole dish. Place the sausages on top of the sauerkraut, then add another layer of sauerkraut. Add the pork chops, then a layer of sauerkraut, repeating until all ingredients are used. Finish with a top layer of sauerkraut. Cover the casserole and bake in the preheated oven for about 1 hour.

Remove the pork chops from the casserole, place around the edge of a serving platter and keep warm. Carefully stir the sauerkraut and sausages together. Taste and adjust the seasonings, adding vinegar or wine if too sweet or sugar if too sour. Return the casserole to the oven for a few more minutes after making adjustments.

To serve, place the sauerkraut and sausages in the center of the warm serving platter. Garnish with parsley and serve with boiled potatoes. *Serves 4.*

Like many artists in the late 19th and early 20th centuries, **Peter Behrens** was concerned that objects produced in factories were being poorly designed. While some designers promoted a return to handmade objects, Behrens was committed to high-quality design in mass-produced goods. Through a long and prolific career, Behrens produced designs for fabrics, furniture, typefaces, and, for the Berlin electrical firm AEG, electrical appliances such as teakettles and fans. This pitcher, produced around 1904 by Westerwald Artpottery, shows Behrens's skill with crisp, geometric forms and rich, but not fussy, decoration.

Like the British Arts and Crafts movement, the Wiener Werkstätte, or Vienna Workshop, aimed to link consumers, designers, and workers through the production of good and simple articles for everyday use. This cruet stand of about 1904, designed by **Koloman Moser**, one of the movement's founders, is at once modest, elegant, and practical—a distinctly modern mix typical of the workshop's best pieces. Objects such as these were mass-produced at the workshop, often in copper or tin; this piece was done in silver, however, adding to its appeal.

GESCHNETZELTES KALBFLEISCH
(Veal in Wine Sauce)

*2 pounds veal leg, shoulder, or breast,
   cut in 2- to 3-inch pieces*
2 teaspoons dried garlic granules
2 tablespoons lemon juice
2 tablespoons vegetable oil
4 tablespoons ($^1/_2$ stick) unsalted butter
1 medium onion, minced
2 tablespoons flour
3 cups chicken stock

$^1/_4$ cup white wine
$^1/_2$ pound mushrooms, sliced
1 garlic clove, minced
$^1/_2$ bay leaf
1 teaspoon sugar
salt and pepper to taste
2 tablespoons sour cream
parsley, minced, for garnish

Preheat the oven to 325°F. Place the veal in a bowl and sprinkle with the garlic granules and lemon juice. Toss to coat evenly. Remove the veal from the bowl and pound lightly with a meat mallet until somewhat flattened.

Heat the oil and butter over high heat in a Dutch oven or ovenproof container with a tight-fitting lid. Lightly brown the veal on all sides. Add the minced onion and cook, stirring, about 2 minutes. Add the flour and stir, cooking for 2 more minutes. Add the remaining ingredients except the sour cream and parsley. Bring the stew to a boil, cover, and place in the oven. Cook until the veal is tender, 1$^1/_2$ to 2 hours.

Remove the stew from the oven and adjust seasonings to taste. If the sauce is too thin, reduce it briefly on the stove. If too thick, add chicken broth or white wine to thin it to the right consistency.

When ready to serve, discard the bay leaf and mix a little of the sauce with the sour cream. Stir the sour cream mixture back into the stew. Do not reheat the stew after adding the sour cream or the sauce may curdle. Serve garnished with minced parsley. *Serves 4 to 6.*

HUHNERSCHNITZEL IN TOMATENSOSSE

(Chicken Schnitzel with Tomato Sauce)

TOMATO SAUCE:

2 tablespoons unsalted butter

1 tablespoon vegetable oil

1 large onion, minced

2 cloves garlic, minced

2 tablespoons flour

one 14-ounce can diced tomatoes with basil

3 tablespoons tomato purée

1½ cups chicken stock

1 packet chicken bouillon granules

1 tablespoon sugar

dash of cayenne pepper (optional)

salt and pepper to taste

CHICKEN SCHNITZEL:

4 boneless, skinless chicken breasts, trimmed

*1 cup no-salt cracker crumbs, finely ground in
    food processor or blender*

½ teaspoon dried basil

¼ teaspoon dried oregano

¼ teaspoon pepper

¼ cup flour

1 large egg

2 tablespoons water

½ cup vegetable oil

2 tablespoons (¼ stick) unsalted butter

parsley, minced, for garnish

Prepare the sauce. Heat the butter and oil over medium heat in large saucepan and sauté the minced onion and garlic for about 5 minutes. Add the flour to the pan and cook, stirring, about 2 minutes. Add the remaining ingredients. Simmer for about 1 hour.

While the sauce simmers, rinse the chicken breasts under cold water and pat dry with paper towels. Using the flat side of a meat mallet, pound the chicken breasts to a uniform thickness. Mix together the cracker crumbs, basil, oregano, and pepper on a plate. Put the flour on a second plate. Break the egg onto a third plate. Add the water to the egg and mix together with a fork. Dredge the chicken breasts in the flour. Dip each breast in the egg mixture, then coat with the cracker crumbs. (The chicken breasts can be prepared up to this point, covered with plastic wrap, and refrigerated several hours ahead.)

Heat the vegetable oil and butter in a large skillet over medium-high heat. Place the chicken breasts in the hot oil and brown each side 3 to 4 minutes, until just thoroughly cooked. Season the tomato sauce to taste. Top the chicken breasts with the sauce and minced parsley and serve. *Serves 4.*

"Ugliness corrupts not only the eyes, but the heart and mind." So said **Henry Van de Velde** of the power of design. The Belgian designer practiced what he preached, designing everything for his family home in Brussels from furniture, silver, cutlery, and the building itself to his wife's clothes. He is said even to have advised her on the color coordination of food served in the house. This plate comes from a tea service van de Velde designed in 1904 or 1905 for the Meissen porcelain factory.

Though architect and designer **Josef Hoffmann** was one of the founders and most important figures of the Wiener Werkstätte, his sterling silver and ivory tea and coffee service, created for the luxury market, is a far cry from the modest, utilitarian objects the Werkstätte was founded to create. The organic motifs of Art Nouveau, an international design style that flourished in Europe and America around the turn of the 20th century, are evident in the finely crafted finials, fluted surfaces, and other decorative details in this outstanding set. These pieces were designed around 1916 and produced in 1922.

APFELTORTE
(Apple Cake with Bourbon Sauce)

CAKE:

4 tablespoons (½ stick) unsalted butter, softened
1 cup sugar
¼ teaspoon salt
1 teaspoon vanilla extract
1 jumbo or 2 small eggs
1 cup flour
1 teaspoon baking soda
½ teaspoon ground cinnamon
⅛ teaspoon freshly grated nutmeg
2 cups peeled, cored, minced Golden Delicious apples
¾ cup chopped pecans
½ cup brown sugar

SAUCE:

8 tablespoons (1 stick) unsalted butter, melted
1¼ cups sugar
¼ teaspoon baking soda
¾ cup whipping cream
1 teaspoon vanilla extract
3 tablespoons bourbon

ROUX:

2 teaspoons unsalted butter, softened
2 teaspoons flour

Preheat the oven to 350°F. Spray the bottom and sides of an 8 x 12-inch cake pan with a nonstick vegetable-oil spray, then coat with butter and flour. Tap out excess flour and set the pan aside.

Make the batter. Cream the butter, sugar, and salt together in a mixer until light and fluffy. Add the vanilla and egg and beat until very light. Mix the flour, baking soda, cinnamon, and nutmeg. Toss with the apples. Fold the mixture into the batter and spoon into the prepared pan. Mix the pecans and brown sugar and sprinkle over the batter. Place the pan into the oven and bake for about 40 minutes.

While the cake is baking, prepare the sauce. Combine the melted butter, sugar, baking soda, and whipping cream in a large saucepan. Bring the mixture to a boil and cook, stirring, until the foam subsides, about 1 to 2 minutes. Remove from heat and stir in the vanilla and bourbon. Set aside.

When the cake is done, remove the pan from the oven and spoon half of the sauce over the hot cake. Set the cake on a rack to cool. Mash the butter and flour together to make the roux. Add the roux to the remaining sauce, bring to a boil, and lower to a simmer, stirring until the sauce becomes thick and creamy.

To serve, cut the cake into 4-inch squares and top with the warm sauce. *Makes one 8 x 12-inch cake. Serves 6.*

In one of the earliest known written texts, a telling of the Sumerian myth of Gilgamesh, it is said that workmen drink "ale and beer...as if they were river water." Beer flows almost as freely in Dutch artist **Adriaen van Ostade**'s *Merrymakers in an Inn*, 1674. While wine remained the beverage of choice for French and Italians, northern Europeans—especially the peasants van Ostade portrayed—preferred ale and beer. By the time this painting was made, the Netherlands was an important brewing center in Europe due to the availability of hops grown there.

When filled with wine or held up to the light, this goblet reveals a diamond-engraved portrait of German Emperor Leopold I. This engraving technique was popular in the 16th and 17th centuries in Germany—so popular that **Georg Schwanhardt the Elder,** to whom the goblet is attributed, gave glass-engraving lessons to Leopold himself. The goblet also features portraits of the four electors of the Holy Roman Empire. A toast to the men pictured on this goblet was a gesture of political solidarity, of hope for German unification—a dream that would not come true for another 200 years.

ALPENKUCHEN
(Chocolate/White-Mousse Cake)

CAKE:

6 ounces semisweet chocolate
12 tablespoons (1 1/2 sticks) butter, softened
5 large egg yolks
3/4 cup sugar
3/4 teaspoon salt
5 egg whites
1 tablespoon cornstarch
1 teaspoon vanilla extract
1 tablespoon orange or raspberry liqueur

WHITE-MOUSSE FILLING:

2 tablespoons cold water
1 1/4 teaspoons unflavored gelatin
3 large egg yolks
1/4 cup brown sugar, packed
1/4 cup water
1/4 teaspoon salt
3 tablespoons Grand Marnier or other liqueur
1 teaspoon vanilla extract
1 cup whipping cream
1/8 teaspoon salt
chopped pecans

Preheat the oven to 340°F. Spray a 10-inch springform pan with a nonstick vegetable-oil spray, then coat with butter and flour. Tap out excess flour and set aside.

Chop the chocolate into small pieces in a food processor or by hand. Put the chocolate into a 4-cup, microwave-safe measuring cup. Melt the chocolate in a microwave on high for 2 minutes. Stir the chocolate, then return to the microwave and heat for 3 minutes on medium power. Stir again and add the softened butter. Heat on low power for about 2 minutes or until the butter and chocolate are melted. Remove and stir until smooth. Place the measuring cup in cold water to cool.

Beat the egg yolks, 1/2 cup of the sugar, and 1/2 teaspoon of the salt together with a mixer until very light and fluffy. Pour into a bowl and set aside.

Wash the mixing bowl and beater and dry thoroughly. Add the egg whites to the bowl. Mix together the remaining 1/4 cup of the sugar, cornstarch, and the remaining 1/4 teaspoon of the salt in a small bowl. Beat the egg whites and gradually add the sugar mixture. Add the vanilla and liqueur and continue to beat until the egg whites hold a stiff peak.

Add the cooled chocolate to the egg yolk mixture and stir until smooth. Carefully fold the egg-white mixture into the chocolate mixture. Immediately pour the batter into the prepared pan. Place the pan on a cookie sheet and bake in the oven for 35 to 40 minutes. The cake will rise to the top of the pan and the edges will crack.

Remove the pan from the oven and cool on a wire rack for 15 minutes. With a knife, cut around the sides of the cake. Place the cake on top of a pot or coffee pan, release the springform pan lock and let the rim fall to the counter. Put the cake back on the cooling rack. The cake will fall in the center as it cools, making room for the mousse. Wash and dry the springform pan rim and, when the cake is cool, clamp it back on the pan. Cover with plastic wrap and refrigerate overnight.

The next day, remove the cake from the refrigerator, remove the springform rim and the cake from the pan bottom, and set the cake on a serving plate.

Make the white-mousse filling. Combine the water and gelatin in a small bowl and set aside. With a whisk, beat the egg yolks, sugar, water, and salt in a small saucepan. Place over very low heat. Using a candy or instant-read thermometer, cook, stirring constantly with the whisk, until the mixture becomes frothy and the thermometer registers about 165°F. (Do not let mixture curdle.) Immediately remove from the heat. Stir in the gelatin and mix until dissolved. Add the vanilla and liqueur and stir. Set the pan in ice water and stir with a whisk until cold. When the mixture has cooled, set it aside, stirring occasionally to prevent it from setting (if it does set, put the pan in hot water and stir to soften).

Put the cream and salt into a mixing bowl. Beat until the cream holds stiff peaks. Using a rubber spatula, fold about ¼ of the whipped cream into the egg yolk-sugar mixture to lighten it and then fold in the remaining cream. Fill the sunken part of the cake to the rim with the mousse. Leave a chocolate edge all around the mousse. Coat the sides of the cake with mousse and refrigerate for at least 8 hours.

Press the chopped pecans onto the sides of the cake, then sweep any excess nuts off the serving plate. Refrigerate until ready to serve.

To serve, cut the cake with a knife dipped into hot water and dried. The cake will keep for about 1 week, refrigerated. *Makes one 10-inch round cake. Serves 8 to 10.*

Belgian designer **Henry Van de Velde** was a central figure in the Art Nouveau movement. Demonstrating his mature style, this samovar, or Russian tea urn, is enlivened by the entwining organic forms of the base and teak handle and the contrasting, simplified form of the kettle. Determined that his designs remain affordable and accessible to a broad public, van de Velde directed that this urn be manufactured of silvered brass rather than of the more luxurious silver.

FOR FURTHER READING

Culinary Art draws on the history and lore of food, but it does not attempt to present a comprehensive survey of the subject. Those in search of such information might start with Maguellone Toussaint-Samat's *History of Food* (Cambridge, Massachusetts, and Oxford, 1992), an interesting, if eccentric, overview. While the book has its shortcomings (one reference to Germany in the index, none to squash), Toussaint-Samat compensates by paying special attention to the symbolic and mythological meanings of food. *American Food: The Gastronomic Story* (New York, 1981) by Evan Jones covers the history of eating on this continent and has the added attraction of a generous selection of historic recipes. In *Food: An Authoritative and Visual History and Dictionary of the Foods of the World* (New York, 1980), Waverly Root digs up at least one tasty fact, and often much more, on just about every food imaginable.

Readers interested in more general writing on food should explore the work of M. F. K. Fisher. She discerned meanings in the acts of cooking and eating that others miss; even in her fiction and memoirs, food has a way of becoming the center of experience. Her translation of Jean Anthelme Brillat-Savarin's *Physiology of Taste* (New York, 1949) is a masterful example of food writing.

Allen J. Grieco's slim survey, *The Meal* (London, 1992), part of Scala Books' series on "Themes in Art," is one of the few general books on the relationship between art and food. In *Feasting: A Celebration of Food and Art* (Chicago, 1992), James Yood discusses 30 paintings of food and feasts in the collection of The Art Institute of Chicago. Two exhibition catalogues, *Art What Thou Eat: Images of Food in American Art* (Mount Kisco, New York, 1991) and *Consuming Passions: The Art of Food and Drink* (Cleveland, 1983), offer other approaches to the subject. When a scholar such as the art historian Robert Rosenblum can produce a serious study such as *The Dog in Art from Rococo to Post-Modernism* (New York, 1988), the lack of books on food and art seems all the more glaring. Graduate students in search of theses, take note.

—Tom Fredrickson

ABOUT THE RESTAURANTS

Restaurants are listed according to the order of chapters.

Bêtise
Plaza del Lago
1515 Sheridan Road
Wilmette, Illinois 60091
(708) 853-1711

From the ruddy cobblestone floors and the lively artwork that covers the walls to the food on the tables, Nancy Barocci's "bistro on the lake" lives up to its name: *bêtise* is French slang for something playful or whimsical. Sitting at the bar during the evening or at a bright table for brunch, it is easy to imagine that Bêtise is located in Provence rather than on Chicago's North Shore. In this cozy setting, the restaurant offers an engaging combination of classic bistro fare and Riviera dishes, often updated with a fresh twist or unexpected pairing.

New Japan
1322 Chicago Avenue
Evanston, Illinois 60201
(708) 475-5980

For 11 years, this cozy, family-owned restaurant has combined *washoku* and *yoshoku*, the Japanese and European styles of cooking. Owners Hisao and Keiko Fukui and partner/chef Hidenori Mukai present time-honored Japanese dishes with a continental flair, offering a wide selection of sushi, sashimi, and noodles, along with succulent sukiyaki and beef teriyaki. Located in Evanston, just a few blocks from Northwestern University, New Japan gives diners a chance to enjoy traditional Japanese food and atmosphere.

Restaurant on the Park
The Art Institute of Chicago
111 South Michigan Avenue
Chicago, Illinois 60603
(312) 443-3543

Known to many as a highlight of visits to The Art Institute of Chicago, Restaurant on the Park offers a stunning setting for elegant continental dining. The spacious, semiformal dining room boasts a breathtaking view of Grant Park and the city and a selection of architectural artifacts from the museum's collection. The restaurant's unusually diverse array of sophisticated dishes, from honey-glazed quail to grilled sea scallops, has made Restaurant on the Park an attraction in its own right as well as a satisfying interlude between gallery visits.

Va Pensiero
1566 Oak Avenue
Evanston, Illinois 60201
(708) 475-7779

Va Pensiero, hidden away in Evanston's historic Margarita Inn, offers splendid northern Italian food in a refined, graceful setting. Its menu features homemade pastas, creative versions of traditional dishes, and an extensive list of fine Italian wines. With the added charm of Romanesque decor, this genteel restaurant is a favorite with lovers of Italian cuisine.

Prairie

The Hyatt on Printers Row
500 South Dearborn Street
Chicago, Illinois 60605
(312) 663-1143

Decorated in the style of the Prairie School, in which architect Frank Lloyd Wright was a leading figure, this "restaurant of the heartland" draws on flavors and foods of the Midwest. Prairie's dishes, like Wright's design, have a traditional, regional character, yet are uniquely modern. Using original recipes and the freshest ingredients to be found in the Midwest, Prairie succeeds in creating innovative dishes that honor and extend the region's culinary heritage.

Frontera Grill

445 North Clark Street
Chicago, Illinois 60610
(312) 661-1434

The lively Frontera Grill serves up the authentic flavors of Mexico in dishes rarely seen north of the Rio Grande. Rick Bayless and Deann Groen Bayless's extensive travels and research in Mexico have inspired them to create meals of complicated, intense seasonings and the freshest ingredients. Recently named by the *International Herald Tribune* as one of the top-ten casual restaurants in the world, Frontera Grill is redefining what a Mexican restaurant can be.

Papagus Greek Taverna

Embassy Suites Hotel
620 North State Street
Chicago, Illinois 60610
(312) 642-8450

The ancient Greek poet Aristophanes noted that thrushes and grasshoppers were prized as delicacies in his day. Happily, restaurateur Rich Melman's Papagus Greek Taverna appeals to more modern tastes. Named "best new restaurant" in Chicago by *Esquire* magazine in 1992, Papagus is Melman's lavish homage to traditional Greek cooking. It boasts a colorful Hellenic interior combining rustic and classical details and a skilled kitchen that dazzles diners with exemplary turns on Greek dishes.

The Berghoff

17 West Adams Street
Chicago, Illinois 60603
(312) 427-3170

For almost 100 years, The Berghoff has been serving hearty German food to diners in Chicago's Loop. Trademark dishes offered at this venerable restaurant—whitefish, sauerbraten, creamed spinach—are legendary. Although its all-male waitstaff is a thing of the past, The Berghoff, with its old-world, wood-paneled atmosphere, sustains a tradition of good solid food and good solid value rare in the late 20th century.

CHECKLIST OF ARTWORKS

Works are listed by chapter and page number

P. 2: *Wine, Cheese, and Fruit*, 1857
John Francis (American, 1808–1886)
Oil on canvas; 25 x 30 in. (63.5 x 76.2 cm)
Restricted gift of Charles C. Haffner III and Mrs. Herbert Vance; and the Wesley M. Dixon, Jr., Fund, 1994.239

P. 6: *Thanksgiving*, c. 1935
Doris Lee (American, 1905–1983)
Oil on canvas; $28\frac{1}{8}$ x 40 in. (71.4 x 101.6 cm)
Mr. and Mrs. Frank G. Logan Prize Fund, 1935.313

FRENCH

P. 9: *The Plate of Apples*, c. 1877
Paul Cézanne (French, 1839–1906)
Oil on canvas; 18 x $21\frac{1}{2}$ in. (45.7 x 54.6 cm)
Gift of Kate L. Brewster, 1949.512

P. 12 (top): *The Checkered Tablecloth*, 1939
Pierre Bonnard (French, 1867–1947)
Oil on canvas; 23 x 23 in. (58.4 x 58.4 cm)
Gift of Mary and Leigh Block, 1988.141.4

P. 12 (bottom): Covered Sugar Bowl
French, 1781
Sèvres Porcelain Manufactory
Hard-paste porcelain, enameling; h. $4\frac{5}{16}$ in. (11 cm), diam. $4\frac{1}{8}$ in. (10.5 cm)
Gift of Mrs. Edgar J. Uihlein through the Antiquarian Society, 1992.633

P. 13 (top): *At the Moulin Rouge*, 1892/1895
Henri de Toulouse-Lautrec (French, 1864–1901)
Oil on canvas; $48\frac{7}{16}$ x $55\frac{1}{2}$ in. (123 x 141 cm)
Helen Birch Bartlett Memorial Collection, 1928.610

P. 13 (bottom): *Still Life with a Basket of Fruit and a Bunch of Asparagus*, 1630
Louise Moillon (French, 1610–1696)
Oil on panel; 21 x $28\frac{1}{8}$ in. (53.3 x 71.4 cm)
Wirt D. Walker Fund, 1948.78

P. 14: *Still Life: Preparation for Lunch*, c. 1940
Pierre Bonnard (French, 1867–1947)
Gouache, with touches of watercolor and graphite, on cream wove paper; $19\frac{1}{2}$ x $25\frac{1}{2}$ in. (49.5 x 656 cm)
Olivia Shaler Swan Memorial Fund, 1943.89

P. 15: *Lorette with a Cup of Coffee*, 1916–1917
Henri Matisse (French, 1869–1954)
Oil on canvas; 26 x $16\frac{15}{16}$ in. (66 x 43 cm)
Estate of Marguerita S. Ritman; Marion and Samuel Klasstorner Endowment; through prior gift of Philip D. Armour and through prior bequests of Dorothy C. Morris and Marguerita S. Ritman, 1993.186

P. 16: *Still Life: Corner of a Table*, 1873
Henri Fantin-Latour (French, 1836–1904)
Oil on canvas; $37\frac{15}{16}$ x $49\frac{3}{16}$ in. (96.4 x 12.5 cm)
Ada Turnbull Hertle Fund, 1951.226

P. 17: *The Rowers' Lunch*, 1875/1876
Pierre Auguste Renoir (French, 1841–1919)
Oil on canvas; $21\frac{11}{16}$ x $25\frac{15}{16}$ in. (55.1 x 65.9 cm)
Potter Palmer Collection, 1922.437

P. 18: Lampwork Fruit Paperweight
French, c. 1848–1855
Compagnie des Cristalleries de Saint-Louis
Blown glass; h. $2\frac{3}{4}$ in. (7 cm)
Bequest of Arthur Rubloff, 1988.541.445

JAPANESE

P. 19: Kimono *(Furisode)*
Japanese, Late Edo period, 19th century
Silk, satin damask weave, *rinzu*; embroidered with silk and gold-leaf-paper-wrapped silk; $72\frac{1}{4}$ x $50\frac{3}{4}$ in. (183.8 x 128.8 cm)
Gift of Gaylord Donnelly in memory of Frances Gaylord Smith, 1991.637

P. 22 (top): Plate
Japanese, Edo period, late 17th century
Arita ware: porcelain with underglaze blue decoration; h. $1\frac{1}{16}$ in. (2.8 cm); diam. $7\frac{5}{8}$ in. (19.4 cm)
Samuel M. Nickerson Endowment, 1976.112

P. 22 (bottom): Bowl
Japanese, Edo Period, late 17th/early 18th century
Arita Ware, Kakiemon style: porcelain with overglaze polychrome enamel decoration; h. $3\frac{5}{8}$ in. (9.3 cm), diam. $7\frac{15}{16}$ in. (20.2 cm)
Gift of the Orientals, 1934.98

P. 23: *The Collections of Famous Beauties: Nakasu*, early 1780s
Torii Kiyonaga (Japanese, 1752–1815)
Woodblock print, diptych; right sheet: $15\frac{1}{4}$ x $10\frac{1}{8}$ in. (38.8 x 25.8 cm); left sheet: $15\frac{5}{16}$ x $10\frac{1}{16}$ in. (39 x 25.5 cm)
Clarence Buckingham Collection, 1925.2295

P. 24: *The Flying Tea Ceremony Kettle (*tonda chagama), c. 1770
Ippitsusai Bunchō (Japanese, active c. 1755–1790)
Woodblock print; $10\frac{13}{16}$ x 8 in. (27.5 x 20.3 cm)
Clarence Buckingham Collection, 1935.384

P. 25: Bottle
Japanese, Edo Period, 17th century
Kutani Ware: porcelain with overglaze enamel decoration; h. $14\frac{1}{8}$ in. (35.9 cm), diam. $7\frac{7}{16}$ in. (18.9 cm)
Samuel M. Nickerson Endowment, 1934.146

P. 26: *View from the Balcony of the Yamashiro Teahouse*, c. 1792
Angyusai Enshi (Japanese, active c. 1785–1795)
Woodblock print, triptych, right and center sheets; complete triptych: $14\frac{3}{4}$ x $28\frac{15}{16}$ in. (37.5 x 73.5 cm)
Clarence Buckingham Collection, 1937.498

P. 27: *Portrait of a Waitress at Izumi-ya Teahouse*, 1790s
Rekisentie Eiri (Japanese, active c. 1790–1800)
Woodblock print; $14\frac{9}{16}$ x $9\frac{7}{8}$ in. (37.1 x 25.1 cm)
Clarence Buckingham Collection, 1942.110

P. 28: Jar
Japanese, Momoyama Period, late 16th century
Iga ware: glazed stoneware; h. 13 in. (33 cm), diam. $9^{5}/_{8}$ in. (24.5 cm)
Through prior gifts of Josephine P. Albright in memory of Alice Higinbotham Patterson, Tiffany Blake, John Carlson, Mrs. Kent S. Clow, Edith Farnsworth, Alfred E. Hamill, and Mrs. Charles S. Potter and Mrs. Hunnewell in memory of Mrs. Freeman Hinkley, 1987.146

P. 29: *Eight Parlor Views: Night Rain at the Tea Ceremony Stand*, c. 1778
Torii Kiyonaga (Japanese, 1752–1815)
Woodblock print; $10^{1}/_{4}$ x $7^{3}/_{4}$ in. (26 x 19.7 cm)
Clarence Buckingham Collection, 1925.2622

CONTINENTAL

P. 31: *At Mouquin's*, 1905
William Glackens (American, 1870–1938)
Oil on canvas; $48^{3}/_{16}$ x $36^{1}/_{4}$ in. (122.4 x 92.1 cm)
Friends of American Art Collection, 1925.295

P. 34: Tureen
English, 1824/1825
John Bridge (1755–1834)
Silver with repoussé, cast, applied, and chased decoration; h. 15 in. (38.1 cm)
Restricted gift of Emily Crane Chadbourne, 1967.486

P. 35: Standing Cup
English, 1607–1608
Anthony Bates (1550–1607)
Silver gilt with repoussé, cast, applied and chased decoration; h. $12^{1}/_{4}$ in. (31.1 cm)
Kate S. Buckingham Jacobean Room Fund, 1972.321

P. 36: *Plattered Fish, Georgia*, 1966
Ivan Le Lorrain Albright (American, 1897–1983)
Gouache, with brush and black ink, on ivory wove clay-coated paper; 16 x 20 in. (40.6 x 50.8 cm)
Gift of the artist, 1977.260

P.37: *A Family Meal*, 1890/1900
Evert Pieter (Dutch, 1856–?)
Oil on canvas; $47^{5}/_{8}$ x $35^{7}/_{16}$ in. (121 x 90 cm)
Gift of Nancy P. Pirie, 1986.1281

P. 38: Coffeepot
English (London), 1900/1901
Designed by Charles Robert Ashbee (1863–1942)
Silver with chrysoprase; $6^{3}/_{16}$ x $7^{1}/_{16}$ x 5 in. (15.7 x 17.9 x 12.7 cm)
Gift of The Antiquarian Society through the Eloise W. Martin Fund in honor of Edith Bruce, 1987.354

P. 39: *Fruits from the Midi*, 1881
Pierre Auguste Renoir (French, 1841–1919)
Oil on canvas; $19^{15}/_{16}$ x $25^{11}/_{16}$ in. (50.7 x 65.3 cm)
Mr. and Mrs. Martin A. Ryerson Collection, 1933.1176

P. 40: *Still Life: Apples and Green Glass*, 1925
Charles Demuth (American, 1883–1935)
Watercolor and graphite, on ivory wove paper; $11^{13}/_{16}$ x $13^{3}/_{4}$ in. (30 x 35 cm)
Gift of Annie Swan Coburn in memory of Olivia Shaler Swan; 1933.473

P. 41: *Renganeschi's, Saturday Night*, 1912
John Sloan (American, 1871–1951)
Oil on canvas; $26^{5}/_{16}$ x $32^{1}/_{8}$ in. (66.8 x 81.6 cm)
Gift of Mary Otis Jenkins, 1926.1580

P. 42 (top): *Cakes No. 1*, 1967
Wayne Thiebaud (American, b. 1920)
Pastel on cream tracing paper; $17^{1}/_{2}$ x $18^{5}/_{8}$ in. (44.5 x 47.4 cm)
Gift of the Society for Contemporary Art, 1971.391

P. 42 (bottom): Tumbler
Probably Netherlandish, 16th century
Blown glass with applied decoration and metal rings; h. $5^{1}/_{4}$ in. (13.3 cm)
Gift of Julius and Augusta N. Rosenwald, 1927.1282

ITALIAN

P. 43: *Kitchen Still Life*, c. 1640
Paolo Antonio Barbieri (Italian, 1603–1649)
Oil on canvas; $26^{1}/_{8}$ x $31^{3}/_{16}$ in. (66.4 x 79.2 cm)
A. A. Munger Collection, 1934.389

P. 46: Ewer
Italian (Florence), 1755/1765
Doccia Porcelain Factory
Hard-paste porcelain with enameling and gilding; h. $11^{1}/_{16}$ in. (29 cm)
Harry and Maribel G. Blum Foundation Endowment, Annette M. Chapin Endowment, 1988.269

P. 47 (top): Wine Cistern
Italian, 1553
Painted by Francesco Durantino (active 1543–1553)
Tin-glazed earthenware (maiolica); $10^{1}/_{4}$ x $20^{1}/_{4}$ x $16^{1}/_{4}$ in. (26 x 51.4 x 41.3 cm)
Anonymous Fund, 1966.395

P. 47 (bottom): Pilgrim Bottle
Italian (Urbino), 1575–1600
Tin-glazed earthenware; $13^{15}/_{16}$ x $11^{1}/_{2}$ in. (35.3 x 29.2 cm)
Buckingham Fund, 1941.821

P. 48 (top): Footed Bowl
Roman (probably from Syria), 4th/5th century A.D.
Blown glass with tooled rim and applied foot; $2^{5}/_{16}$ x $6^{11}/_{16}$ in. (7.4 x 16.9 cm)
Gift of Theodore W. and Frances S. Robinson, 1945.670

P. 48 (bottom): Knob-Handled Dish
Greek (from Apulia, Italy), 330/320 B.C.
The Baltimore Painter
Earthenware, red-figure technique; diam. $26^{5}/_{8}$ in. (67 cm)
Katherine K. Adler Fund, 1984.10

P. 49: Jug
Roman, late 1st/early 3rd century A.D.
Blown glass with applied and tooled handle; h. $5^{1}/_{2}$ in. (13.9 cm)
Gift of Theodore W. and Frances S. Robinson, 1949.1132

P. 50: Ewer and Basin
Italian, c. 1745
Attributed to Giuseppe Gricci (1743–1760)
Capodimonte Porcelain Manufactory, Naples
Soft-paste porcelain with enameling and gilding, ewer: h. 12 in. (30.5 cm), basin: $6^{1}/_{2}$ x $15^{1}/_{4}$ x $13^{1}/_{2}$ in. (16.5 x 38.4 x 34.3 cm)
Gift of Mr. and Mrs. Robert Norman Chatain in memory of Professor Alfred Chatain, 1957.490

P. 51: Stemmed Bowl with Lid (*Lebes*)
Etruscan (possibly from Vulci), Geometric Period, 725/700 B.C.
Earthenware; $22\frac{7}{16}$ x $16\frac{15}{16}$ in. (57 x 43 cm)
Costa A. Pandaleon Fund, 1985.627

P. 52: *The Marriage at Cana*, c. 1686
Giuseppe Maria Crespi (Italian, 1665–1747)
Oil on canvas; 74 x $97\frac{3}{4}$ in. (188 x 248.3 cm)
Wirt D. Walker Fund, 1956.129

P. 53: Water Jar Used as a Funerary Vessel (*Loutrophorous*)
Greek (from Apulia, Italy), c. 365 B.C.
The Varrese Painter
Earthenware, red-figure technique; h. $34\frac{5}{8}$ in. (88 cm)
Katherine K. Adler Fund, 1984.9

AMERICAN

P. 55: *For To Be a Farmer's Boy*, 1887
Winslow Homer (American, 1836–1910)
Watercolor with touches of scraping over graphite, on cream wove paper; 14 x 20 in. (35.5 x 50.9 cm)
Anonymous gift in memory of Edward Carson Waller, 1963.760

P. 58: Pitcher
American (New York), 1878
Tiffany & Co.
Silver, gold, and copper; h. $8\frac{3}{4}$ in. (21 cm), diam. at base $5\frac{1}{2}$ in. (14 cm)
Restricted gift of Mrs. Frank L. Sulzberger, 1984.240

P. 59 (top): *Walking the Line*, 1835
William Sidney Mount (American, 1807–1868)
Oil on canvas; $22\frac{5}{8}$ x $27\frac{7}{16}$ in. (57.5 x 69.8 cm)
The Goodman Fund, 1939.392

P. 59 (bottom): *Just Dessert*, 1891
William Michael Harnett (American, 1848–1892)
Oil on canvas; $22\frac{1}{4}$ x $26\frac{3}{4}$ in. (56.5 x 68 cm)
Friends of American Art Collection, 1942.50

P. 60: *Blue Crab*, 1977
Jack Beal (American, b. 1931)
Color linocut on cream wove paper; 9 x 12 in. (22.8 x 30.7 cm)
Gift of Allan Frumkin, 1978.556

P. 61 (top): Chocolate Pot
American (Boston), 1847/1851
Jones, Ball & Poor (George B. Jones, True M. Ball, Nathanial C. Poor)
Silver, $4\frac{11}{16}$ x 7 in. (12 x 17.8 cm)
Americana Fund, 1987.130

P. 61 (bottom): *The Café*, c. 1890
Fernand Lungren (American, 1859–1932)
Oil on canvas; $31\frac{3}{8}$ x $41\frac{1}{4}$ in. (79.7 x 102.2 cm)
Charles H. and Mary F. S. Worcester Collection, 1947.85

P. 62 (top): *Strawberries, Nuts, &c.*, 1822
Raphaelle Peale (American, 1774–1825)
Oil on wood panel; $16\frac{3}{8}$ x $22\frac{3}{4}$ in. (41.6 x 57.8 cm)
Gift of Jamee J. and Marshall Field, 1991.100

P. 62 (bottom): Tea Service
American (Brooklyn, N.Y.), 1870/1873
E. G. Webster and Son
Silver plate; coffeepot h. $11\frac{3}{4}$ in. (29.9 cm); milk pot h. 6 in. (15.2 cm); sugar basin h. 9 in. (22.9 cm)
Gift of Mrs. Julian A. Altman, 1989.436.1, .2a-b, and .3.

P. 63: *Thanksgiving*, c. 1935
Doris Lee (American, 1905–1983)
Oil on canvas; $28\frac{1}{8}$ x 40 in. (71.4 x 101.6 cm)
Mr. and Mrs. Frank G. Logan Prize Fund, 1935.313

P. 64 (top): *Still Life with Pineapple, Grapes, Pears, Crabapples, and Strawberries*, 1979
Barnet Rubenstein (American, b. 1923)
Colored pencils and graphite, on off-white wove paper, $22\frac{1}{2}$ x $30\frac{1}{16}$ in. (57.4 x 76.7 cm)
Gift of Jalane and Richard Davidson, 1990.511.5

P. 64 (bottom): Two-Handled Cup with Cover
American (New York), 1698/1720
Cornelius Kierstede (1675–1757)
Silver; h. $5\frac{1}{2}$ in. (14 cm), diam. (top) $5\frac{9}{16}$ in. (14.1 cm)
Restricted gift of Mrs. James W. Alsdorf, Pauline Seipp Armstrong, Marshall Field, Charles C. Haffner III, Mrs. Burton W. Hales, Mrs. Harold T. Martin, Mrs. C. Phillip Miller, Mr. and Mrs. Milo M. Naeve, Mrs. Eric Oldberg, Mrs. Frank L. Sulzberger, and the Ethel T. Scarborough Fund, 1984.1132

P. 65: *Purple Plums*, 1895
Cadurcis Plantagenet Ream (American, 1838–1917)
Oil on canvas; 16 x 22 in. (40.6 x 55.9 cm)
Bequest of Catherine M. White, 1899.907

P. 66 (top): *Movement No. 10*, 1917
Marsden Hartley (American, 1877–1943)
Oil on composition board; $15\frac{1}{4}$ x $19\frac{1}{2}$ in. (38.7 x 49.5 cm)
Alfred Stieglitz Collection, 1949.548

P. 66 (bottom): *Eggplant and Plums*, 1922–23
Charles Demuth (American, 1883–1935)
Watercolor, with graphite, on ivory wove paper; $11\frac{7}{8}$ x $18\frac{1}{8}$ in. (30.4 x 45.9 cm)
Olivia Shaler Swan Memorial Collection, 1933.470

MEXICAN

P. 67: Dish
Mexican, Puebla, c. 1840
Tin-glazed earthenware; h. $2\frac{3}{8}$ in. (6 cm), diam. $16\frac{1}{8}$ in. (41 cm)
Gift of Eva Lewis in memory of her husband, Herbert Pickering Lewis, 1923.1473

P. 70: *The Fruit Vendor*, 1943
Rufino Tamayo (Mexican, 1899–1991)
Gouache, over graphite, on white wove paper; $29\frac{1}{16}$ x $22\frac{15}{16}$ in. (73.8 x 58.2 cm)
Bequest of Mrs. Gilbert W. Chapman, 1981.151

P. 71: *Ready for the Fiesta*, 1920
William Penhallow Henderson (American, 1877–1943)
Oil on cardboard; 40 x 32 in. (101.6 x 81.3 cm)
Gift of Mrs. E. Harrison Rooney, Mrs. George S. Swope, and Mrs. Richard D. Stevenson, 1985.447

P. 72 (top): Bowl Representing an *Achira* Root
Peruvian (South Coast), Nazca culture, 180 B.C./A.D. 500
Ceramic, $6\frac{7}{8}$ x 6 in. (17.5 x 15.2 cm)
Buckingham Fund, 1955.2083

P. 72 (bottom): Storage Jar *(Olla)*
American, Anasazi Culture, c. 1100
Black and white mineral paint on clay, Black Mesa style; 17 x 18 in. (43.2 x 45.7 cm)
Tillie C. Cohn Fund, 1976.307

P. 73: Large Jar
Mexican, Puebla, 1700/1750
Tin-glazed earthenware; h. 24⅜ in. (62 cm), diam.
15⅜ in. (54 cm)
Gift of Eva Lewis in memory of her husband,
Herbert Pickering Lewis, 1923.1443

P. 74: Dish with Fish and Chili Peppers
Peruvian (probably vicinity of Cuzco), Inca culture,
A.D. 1400/1532
Ceramic; 3¹/₁₆ x 9⅜ in. (7.8 x 23.9 cm)
Buckingham Fund, 1955.2223

P. 75: Village Festival Scene
Mexican, Nayarit Culture, c. A.D. 200
Ceramic; 18½ x 13 in. (47 x 33 cm)
Gift of Dr. and Mrs. Julian R. Goldsmith, 1989.639

P. 76 (top): Vessel in the Form of a Squash
Mexican (West Central Region), Colima Culture,
c. A.D. 200
Ceramic; h. 9⅛ in. (23.1 cm), diam. 12¾ in.
(32.4 cm)
John Simpson Fund, 1989.208

P. 76 (bottom): Ceremonial Basket with
Cosmological Designs
North American (Arizona, possibly Salt River
Canyon), Western Apache People, c. 1910
Plant fibers; diam. 23⅛ in. (58.7 cm)
Gift of the family of Rene d'Harnoncourt in
memory of Malcolm Collier and Leslie Denman,
1986.1361

P. 77: Seated Female Figure
Mexican, Colima culture, c. A.D. 400
Ceramic with traces of negative-resist painting;
21 x 13¾ x 10 in. (53 x 35 x 25 cm)
Gift of Mrs. Everett McNear in memory of her
husband, 1986.1088

P. 78: *Vase of the Dancing Lords*
Guatemalan, Maya culture, A.D. 750/800
Earthenware with pigmented clay slip; h. 9½ in.
(24 cm), diam. 6¾ in. (17 cm)
Ethel T. Scarborough Fund, 1986.1081

P. 79: Bowl with Fresco Decorations
Mexican, Teotihuacan Culture, A.D. 300/600
Ceramic, mineral pigment, and lime plaster;
diam. 8⅞ in. (22.5 cm)
Primitive Art Purchase Fund, 1968.790

GREEK

P. 81: Drinking Vessel *(Rhyton)* in the Shape of a
Donkey Head
Greek (Attica), c. 460 B.C.
Painted by Douris
Molded earthenware, red-figure technique; h. 7⅞
in. (20 cm), diam. 3¹¹/₁₆ in. (9.3 cm)
Museum Purchase Fund, 1905.345

P. 84 (top): Water Jar *(Hydria)*
Greek (Attica), 460/450 B.C.
The Leningrad Painter
Earthenware, red-figure technique; h. 16¾ in.
(42.4 cm), diam. 4¹/₁₆ in. (10.3 cm)
Gift of Martin A. Ryerson, 1911.456

P. 84 (bottom): Necklace
Greek (probably from Greek coast of Asia Minor or
from Lydia), possibly 6th century B.C.
Gold and amber; l. 10¹/₁₆ in. (25.5 cm)
Gift of Mrs. T. B. Blackstone, 1905.330

P. 85: Female Figure
Greek (Cycladic Islands), 2600/2400 B.C.
Marble; 15¾ x 4⁹/₁₆ in. (39.6 x 11.5 cm)
Katherine K. Adler Fund, 1978.115

P. 86: Oil Bottle *(Lekythos)*
Greek (Attica), 450/440 B.C.
The Achilles Painter
Earthenware, white-ground technique; h. 12⅛ in.
(30.8 cm), diam. 2⅜ in. (6.0 cm)
Gift of Martin A. Ryerson, 1907.20

P. 87: *The Wedding of Peleus and Thetis*, 1636
Peter Paul Rubens (Flemish, 1577–1640)
Oil on panel; 10¾ x 16⅞ in. (27.3 x 42.9 cm)
Charles H. and Mary F. S. Worcester Collection,
1947.108

P. 88 (top): Fish Plate
Greek (Attica), 400/350 B.C.
Earthenware, red-figure technique; h. 2 in.
(5.1 cm), diam. 13⅜ in. (34 cm)
Gift of Philip D. Armour and Charles L.
Hutchinson, 1889.98

P. 88 (bottom): Covered Dish *(Lekanis)*
Greek (Attica), 480/450 B.C.
Earthenware with black glaze; h. 5 in. (12.7 cm),
diam. 15½ in. (39.4 cm)
Gift of Charles L. Hutchinson, 1889.99

P. 89: Pitcher *(Oinochoe)* in the Shape of a
Female Head
Greek (Attica), 480/460 B.C.
Molded earthenware, red-figure technique;
5⁷/₁₆ x 2¹¹/₁₆ in. (13.8 x 6.8 cm)
Museum Purchase Fund, 1905.348

P. 90 (top): Storage Jar *(Amphora)*
Greek (Attica), 550/525 B.C.
The Painter of Tarquinia RC 3984
Earthenware, black-figure technique; h. 10¾ in.
(28.2 cm), diam. 5 in. (12.7 cm)
Katherine K. Adler Fund, 1978.114

P. 90 (bottom): Drinking Cup *(Kylix)*
Greek (Attica), c. 480 B.C.
Close to the style of the painter Douris
Greek inscription: Hippodamakalos
("Hippodamas is handsome")
Earthenware, red-figure technique; h. 2⅞ in.
(7.3 cm), diam. 8 in. (20.3 cm)
Gift of Martin A. Ryerson, 1907.323

P. 91 (top): Unguent bottles
Eastern Mediterranean or Italian, mid-4th/early
3rd century B.C.
Core-formed glass with applied rim-disks, handles,
pad-base, and thread decoration; maximum dimen-
sions 2¾ x 1⅞ in. (6.9 x 4.7 cm)
Gift of Theodore W. and Frances S. Robinson,
1942.628, 1942.631

P. 91 (bottom): Coin showing a Double
Cornucopia
Greek (from Alexandria, Egypt), after 270 B.C.
Gold octadrachm; diam. 1⅛ in. (2.8 cm)
Gift of Martin A. Ryerson, 1922.4934

GERMAN

P. 93: *Still Life*, c. 1630
Pieter Claesz (Dutch, 1597/1598–1661)
Oil on panel; $18\frac{7}{8}$ x $30\frac{1}{4}$ in. (47.9 x 76.8 cm)
Simeon B. Williams Fund, 1935.300

P. 96: Plate
Czech (Bohemia), c. 1600
Dark-blue glass, diamond-point engraved decoration; h. $1\frac{1}{4}$ in. (3.2 cm), diam. $8\frac{3}{8}$ in. (21.3 cm)
Gift of Julius and Augusta N. Rosenwald, 1927.1271

P. 97: Tall Beaker *(Humpen)*
Czech (Bohemia), c. 1600
Blown glass with polychrome enamel; h. $12\frac{3}{16}$ in. (31 cm), diam. $5\frac{1}{4}$ in. (13.3 cm)
Gift of Julius and Augusta N. Rosenwald, 1927.1012

P. 98: Coffee Service
Austrian, 1901/1902
Designed by Jutta Sika (1877–1964)
Made by Wiener Porzellan-Manufaktur Jos. Böck, Vienna
Hard-paste porcelain with stenciled decoration; teapot and lid (with lid): $6\frac{3}{4}$ x $7\frac{3}{4}$ x $5\frac{3}{16}$ in. (17.1 x 19.7 x 13.2 cm); creamer: $3\frac{3}{8}$ x $4\frac{1}{8}$ x $3\frac{1}{4}$ in. (8.6 x 10.5 x 8.3 cm); tea cup: $2\frac{3}{16}$ x $4\frac{3}{16}$ x $3\frac{5}{16}$ in. (5.5 x 10.6 x 8.4 cm); saucer: h. $1\frac{3}{16}$ in. (3 cm), diam. $6\frac{5}{16}$ in. (16 cm); sugar bowl and lid (with lid): h. $4\frac{7}{16}$ in. (11.3 cm), diam. $4\frac{1}{8}$ in. (10.5 cm)
Gift of the Antiquarian Society through the 1986 New York Trip Fund, 1986.1092-96

P. 99: Pitcher
German, c. 1904
Designed by Peter Behrens (1869–1940)
Westerwald Artpottery
Glazed stoneware; h. $10\frac{1}{2}$ in. (26.7 cm)
Gift of the Antiquarian Society through the Mrs. Edgar J. Uihlein Fund, 1991.314

P. 100: Cruet Stand
Austrian, 1904/1905
Designed by Koloman Moser (1868–1918)
Made by Alfred Mayer, silversmith for the Wiener Werkstätte, Vienna
Silver and glass; stand: $16\frac{11}{16}$ x $5\frac{13}{15}$ x $2\frac{11}{16}$ in. (17 x 14.8 x 6.8 cm); cruets: h. $3\frac{15}{16}$ in. (10 cm), diam. $2\frac{3}{16}$ in. (5.6 cm)
Richard T. Crane Endowment; restricted gift of Mrs. Julian Armstrong, Jr., Mrs. George B. Young, 1987.219.1-3

P. 101: Plate
German, 1904/1905
Designed by Henry Van de Velde (Belgian, 1863–1957)
Meissen Porcelain Manufactory
Hard-paste porcelain with underglaze blue decoration, diam. $10\frac{1}{4}$ in. (26 cm)
Gift of the Antiquarian Society, 1988.34

P. 102: Tea and Coffee Service
Austrian, 1922 (designed c. 1916)
Designed by Josef Hoffmann (1870–1956)
Made by the Wiener Werkstätte, Vienna
Silver and ivory; tray: $1\frac{1}{4}$ x $15\frac{5}{16}$ x $13\frac{1}{2}$ in. (3.2 x 39 x 34.3 cm); coffeepot: $6\frac{1}{8}$ x 8 x $3\frac{15}{16}$ in. (15.5 x 20.3 x 9.9 cm); teapot: $4\frac{7}{16}$ x $10\frac{1}{4}$ x $5\frac{13}{16}$ in. (11.2 x 26 x 14.7 cm); creamer: $2\frac{3}{16}$ x $6\frac{3}{4}$ x $3\frac{13}{16}$ in. (5.6 x 17.1 x 9.6 cm); sugar bowl with lid: $4\frac{15}{16}$ x $4\frac{1}{2}$ x $4\frac{1}{4}$ in. (12.5 x 11.4 x 10.8 cm); sugar tongs: $\frac{7}{8}$ x $5\frac{3}{16}$ x $1\frac{1}{4}$ in. (2.2 x 13.2 x 3.2 cm)
Gift of the Antiquarian Society through the Eloise W. Martin Fund in memory of Mrs. Alfred Collins, 1987.213.1-6

P. 103: *Merrymakers in an Inn*, 1674
Adriaen van Ostade (Dutch, 1610–1684)
Oil on panel, $18\frac{3}{8}$ x $16\frac{1}{8}$ in. (46.7 x 41 cm)
George B. and Mary R. Harris Fund, 1894.1028

P. 104: Goblet
German (Nuremberg), c. 1660
Attributed to Georg Schwanhardt the Elder (1601–1667)
Blown glass with diamond-point engraving; h. $14\frac{3}{8}$ in. (36.5 cm), diam. $5\frac{3}{4}$ in. (14.6 cm)
Gift of Julius and Augusta N. Rosenwald, 1927.1255

P. 105: Samovar
German, 1902–1903
Designed by Henry Van de Velde (Belgian, 1863–1957), manufactured at Theodore Müller, Weimar
Silvered brass, teak; h. $14\frac{7}{8}$ in. (37.9 cm)
Gift of the Historical Design Collection and an anonymous donor; Mr. and Mrs. F. Lee Wendell, European Decorative Arts Purchase funds; Edward E. Ayer Endowment in memory of Charles L. Hutchinson, Bessie Bennett Endowment; through prior gifts of Walter C. Clark, Mrs. Oscar Klein, Mrs. R. W. Morris, Mrs. I. Newton Perry; through prior acquisition of European Decorative Arts Purchase funds, 1989.154

FOOD INDEX

Culinary Art
Recipes from Great Chicago Restaurants

Design concept by Susan Stirling, Oak Park, Illinois
Design and typesetting by Paul Baker Typography, Inc., Chicago,
with the assistance of Sam Silvio Design, Chicago
Typeset in Linotype Garamond 3
Color separations by Professional Graphics, Rockford, Illinois
Printed in an edition of 12,500 by CS Graphics, Singapore,
on 100 lb. Leykam matte